Making It Big

Making It Big

Why Developing Countries Need More Large Firms

Andrea Ciani, Marie Caitriona Hyland,
Nona Karalashvili, Jennifer L. Keller,
Alexandros Ragoussis, and Trang Thu Tran

WORLD BANK GROUP

ISBN (paper): 978-1-4648-1557-7
ISBN (electronic): 978-1-4648-1558-4
DOI: 10.1596/978-1-4648-1557-7

Interior and cover design and cover image: Sergio Andres Moreno Tellez

The Library of Congress Control Number: 2020943028

Contents

Figures

Tables

Foreword

It is no secret: small and mid-size firms are the backbone of economies everywhere. They account for more than 9 out of every 10 businesses. They generate half of all jobs. Yet the actual trajectory of economic growth and prosperity is determined by a different type of firm—businesses lucky or plucky enough to make it big.

High-performing economies tend to have a larger share of employment in big, competitive firms than other countries. Such firms are usually more productive and have better market intelligence: they can lower production costs while making high-quality investments and reaching the markets they need to succeed. They are more likely to innovate, more likely to export, and more likely to adopt international standards of quality. They typically pay higher wages and provide more secure employment than small firms.

In small and lower-income countries, however, there is a pronounced shortage of large, competitive firms—and the deficiency impedes economic progress where it is needed most. Indonesia, for example, has just 9 large firms for every 100 mid-size firms in the nonagricultural sector. By contrast, the United States has 20 large firms for the same number of mid-size firms. If Indonesia's business environment were as friendly to large-firm creation as the business environments of high-income economies, the country could have an estimated 230,000 additional jobs in the manufacturing sector.

This book constitutes one of the most up-to-date assessments of how large firms are created in low- and middle-income countries and what their role is in development. Although the analysis was prepared before the COVID-19 outbreak, its findings are even more relevant in the current context. Productive large firms will play a key role restoring growth and creating jobs in the aftermath of the pandemic.

The book focuses on firms with at least 100 employees. Globally, fewer than 1 out of every 20 firms operates at that scale. In low- and middle-income countries, however, smaller firms face tougher odds of making the big leagues. They stay small; across low- and middle-income countries, only 1 in 10 small firms grows to medium size, and only 1 in 100 grows to become a large firm.

Large firms in these countries, by contrast, are often born big. They also tend to enjoy considerably more regulatory protection than large firms in high-income economies, to the detriment of smaller firms and new entrants to the market.

The superstars among them play an outsized role in many low- and middle-income countries. In Serbia, for example, the 20 largest firms account for more than 5 percent of national employment and 20 percent of GDP. In Ethiopia, the largest manufacturing firm accounts for close to 10 percent of GDP. In Vietnam, the top 20 firms employ more than 1 percent of the country's workforce.

Development is not just about the number of jobs. It is also about better jobs. It is about health, security, efficient use of resources, quality standards, global integration, and resilience. Large firms tend to offer all of these benefits. New, large firms—such as those that challenge the dominance of existing large firms—offer even better prospects.

Progress in these countries, in short, cannot occur without a significant role for new, large firms. The question for policy makers is what can be done to enable more smaller firms to make it big—and what must be done to keep large firms from becoming monopolies. The recommendations of this study offer a way forward. Policy makers should focus on five types of interventions.

First, open up markets. As this study highlights, three private agents play a key role in creating large firms in low- and middle-income countries: multinational companies that establish local affiliates, entrepreneurs that grow their start-ups or create large firms, and large domestic firms that create spinoffs. High-productivity firms that have the ability to grow large deserve the opportunity to do so. Domestic markets should be opened to broad-based competition—through international trade and investment and through policies to ease entry and break up oligopolies. Most countries have a long way to go in this regard; regulatory protection of incumbents is more than 60 percent greater in low- and middle-income countries than it is in high-income countries.

Second, improve the business environment. Costs resulting from government policies—involving courts, labor laws, taxation, and trade rules and customs—can sway investors' decisions regarding where to establish new, large firms and whether to expand. Improving the business environment—through smarter government regulation, stronger trade facilitation, and better protection of property rights—can make a big difference in fostering the emergence of large firms.

Third, avoid state ownership beyond key public goods. Governments have historically created large firms in the form of state-owned enterprises (SOEs)—a generally unproductive exercise. These firms rarely deliver the benefits one might expect, given their scale. Their record of underperformance means that it is hard to establish an independent governance structure that allows them to operate on fully commercial terms. As a rule, governments have also proved unable to manage the conflicts of interest inherent in exposing SOEs to market competition while avoiding financial and job losses. As a result, SOEs rarely emulate the productivity and dynamism of privately owned firms.

Fourth, strengthen private sector capabilities. A dynamic private sector depends on much more than finance. Governments should strive to ensure that private actors—entrepreneurs, foreign investors, and other large firms—have the skills, technology, market intelligence, infrastructure, and finance they need to create large ventures. Development finance institutions should do the same: they can work proactively with lead investors to help them overcome the constraints that dissuade them from creating large ventures—among other things, managerial capabilities and the ability to export and connect to regional and global supply chains.

Fifth, spread the benefits. The propensity of large firms to innovate and achieve higher productivity can generate significant benefits for other firms: large firms create demand in their supply chains, they grow markets, and they spread know-how in ways that benefit other companies of all sizes. Development finance institutions also play an important role here; many, including the International Finance Corporation, have undertaken extensive financing and capacity-building activities to support the growth of high-potential small and medium enterprises. Through such activities, development institutions can help to ensure that the benefits of large-firm growth reach other firms as well.

Low- and middle-income economies have much to gain by enabling more firms to make it big—and it is possible for them to do so without creating monopolies. They should not shirk from the opportunity.

Caroline Freund
Global Director for Trade, Investment, and Competitiveness
World Bank Group

Acknowledgments

This book was prepared jointly by the International Finance Corporation (IFC), the Development Economics Group (DEC), and the Equitable Growth, Finance, and Institutions (EFI) Vice Presidency of the World Bank Group; and the Productivity and Business Dynamics Division of the Organisation for Economic Co-operation and Development (OECD).

The preparation of the book was managed by Neil Gregory and led by Alexandros Ragoussis in the Economics and Private Sector Development Vice Presidency of IFC. The report team included Andrea Ciani (chapter 2), Marie Caitriona Hyland (chapter 1), Nona Karalashvili (chapter 1), Jennifer L. Keller (chapter 4), Alexandros Ragoussis (chapters 2 and 4), and Trang Thu Tran (chapters 1 and 3). Valuable analytical inputs were contributed by Reyes Aterido, Miriam Bruhn, Massimiliano Cali, Flavio Calvino, Tania Ghossein, Sarah Waltraut Hebous, Ayanda Hlatshwayo, Hibret Maemir, Mulalo Mamburu, Tristan Reed, Adrian Scutaru, Jonathan Timmis, and James Tybout. The team is grateful to Rahma Ahmed, Nisan Gorgulu, Mengxi Jin, Kevin Matthees, and Chinemelu Okafor for research assistance; to Susan Graham, Patricia Katayama, and Yaneisy Martinez for managing the book's publication; and to Stephanie Evergreen for the design of charts and graphs.

Helpful discussions and guidance at various stages of the manuscript's preparation were provided by Eric Bartelsman, Giuseppe Berlingieri, Paddy Carter, Deepa Chakrapani, Chiara Criscuolo, David Francis, Caroline Freund, Alvaro Gonzalez, Tanja Goodwin, Arti Grover Goswami, Shafik Hebous, Asif Islam, Hans Peter Lankes, Philippe Le Houérou, Martha Martinez Licetti, Alex MacGillivray, Denis Medvedev, Dino Merotto, Joseph Rebello, Bob Rijkers, Jorge Rodriguez Meza, Sylvia Solf, John Sutton, and Christopher Woodruff. Likewise, participants in two technical workshops (one held in London and the other in Washington, DC) and in research seminars at the University of Oxford, CDC, and the European Bank for Reconstruction and Development provided valuable inputs.

Executive Summary

Economic and social progress requires a diverse ecosystem of firms of different sizes playing complementary roles. This report focuses on the particular role that larger firms—defined as firms with 100 employees or more—play in this ecosystem. Fewer than 1 out of 20 enterprises operates at this scale across the world.

This report shows that large firms are different than other firms in low- and middle-income countries. They are significantly more likely to innovate, export, and offer training and are more likely to adopt international standards of quality. Their particularities are closely associated with productivity advantages—that is, their ability to lower the costs of production through economies of scale and scope but also to invest in quality and reach demand. Across low- and middle-income countries with available business census data, nearly 6 out of 10 large enterprises are also the most productive in their country and sector.

These distinct features of large firms translate into improved outcomes not only for their owners but also for their workers and for smaller enterprises in their value chains. Workers in large firms report, on average, 22 percent higher hourly wages in household and labor surveys from 32 low- and middle-income countries—a premium that rises considerably in lower-income contexts. That is partly because large firms attract better workers. But this is not the only reason: accounting for worker characteristics and nonpecuniary benefits, the large-firm wage premium remains close to 15 percent. Besides higher wages—which are strongly associated with higher productivity—large firms more frequently offer formal jobs, secure jobs, and nonpecuniary benefits such as health insurance that are fundamental for welfare in low- and middle-income countries.

Large firms represent important vehicles of change by contributing to an important share of net job creation and labor productivity growth across different contexts—more than 50 percent across the sample of countries for which we have both firm-level and macroeconomic data. A handful of top performers lead the way; the 20 largest firms in Vietnam, Côte d'Ivoire, and Serbia contribute, respectively, more than 10, 15, and 50 percent of total tax revenue on profits and capital gains. In Côte d'Ivoire and Serbia, these 20 firms account for more than half of total national exports.

The fundamental challenge for economic development, however, is that production does not reach economic scale in low- and middle-income countries.

Smaller and lower-income markets tend to host smaller firms. But even in relative terms, there are too few larger firms in these countries relative to the size of the economy and the number of smaller firms—there is a "missing top." In 2016, for example, for every 100 medium-size firms, more than 20 large firms were operating in the nonagricultural sector in the United States, as opposed to less than 9 in Indonesia—a lower-middle-income country with roughly the same population. A closer study of the firm-size distribution in country pairs suggests that what is missing are the larger of large firms—that is, those with 300+ employees—as well as the more productive and outward-oriented firms. The observation that relatively less distorted economies have smoother firm-size distributions allows us to examine the hypothesis based also on some theoretical shape that better fits less distorted economies, such as the Pareto distribution. The evidence suggests that larger firms employing more than 300 workers are systematically underrepresented in the lower-income countries under observation. In Ethiopia, for example, large firms have a 7-percentage-point lower share of employment than what is predicted by the optimal distribution, while in Indonesia, the gap is 4.6 percentage points, corresponding to a rough estimate of 230,000 missing jobs in manufacturing.

The scarcity of larger firms raises the question of how larger firms are created in lower-income contexts and what goes wrong in this process. Firms begin with "sponsors" that combine capital, labor, and know-how, in order to access a market or create a new one. Four types of sponsors predominate in lower-income countries: foreign firms creating new affiliates, other large firms spinning off new ventures, governments, and entrepreneurs. These four actors have different advantages in bringing together the ingredients of a successful enterprise—capital, labor, technology, managerial talent, and market access—and often build on existing assets and experience to create new ventures. As a result, what is distinct about large firms is often in place from the time they are established.

Drawing on a rare set of firm-level data from public and private sources, as well as proprietary data from the International Finance Corporation (IFC) and case studies, this report shows that large firms are often born large—or with attributes of largeness in the way they are organized, their strategies for market access, and the people they engage as managers and workers. Firms that grow large from smaller sizes and those that start off large, for example, both pay between 25 and 50 percent higher wages than the rest at origin. They also report, on average, one additional layer of employment at origin. In the manufacturing sector of large countries such as China, Indonesia, and Vietnam, large firms more often originate from the same segment: 55 to 80 percent of large firms are estimated to have started off large. Of the large firms appraised by IFC between 2015 and 2017, two out of three were also large at origin. The evidence highlights the critical role of ex ante capabilities, including the intelligence to access and expand demand, in explaining the growth of firms in low- and middle-income countries.

To fill the "missing top," governments have often resorted to the creation of state-owned enterprises (SOEs). These firms rarely deliver the benefits one might expect from their scale. First, it has proven difficult to establish governance sufficiently independent of the state to operate in a commercial manner. SOEs often pursue a mix of social and commercial objectives, which are used to justify regulatory protection from competition. It is also difficult for governments to manage the conflict of interest that arises between exposing SOEs to competition, on the one hand, and the risk of job losses and changes in product offerings that come with this exposure, on the other. As a result, SOEs in lower-income economies rarely emulate the productivity and dynamism of privately owned firms: they are three times less likely to be the most productive firm in their country and sector.

Instead of that course of action, this report argues strongly that governments should support the creation of new, large firms through private investment by opening up markets to competition. In low-income countries, governments can achieve that objective with simple policy reorientations, such as breaking oligopolies, removing unnecessary restrictions to international trade and investment, and putting in place strong competition frameworks to prevent the abuse of market power. Opening markets to competition benefits entrants of all sizes. In practice, however, regulation is often designed for the benefit of large incumbents using statutory monopolies and oligopolies, preferential access to natural resources and government contracts, or barriers to foreign competitors that rarely enter at small scale in new markets. The entry of more large firms to compete with incumbents would aim to disperse power by any one firm. There is a long way to go in this regard: regulatory protection of incumbents in lower-middle-income countries is more than 60 percent greater, on average, than the level observed in high-income countries.

Beyond the entry point, operational costs associated with a range of government policies can greatly influence investors' decisions to establish new, large firms. Large firms in low- and middle-income countries are significantly more likely than small firms to report customs operations, the court system, workforce skills, transportation, and telecommunications infrastructure as constraining their operations. Bread-and-butter reforms that aim to improve market regulation, trade processes, and tax regimes and to protect intellectual property rights stand to make a difference in that respect, even when these long-term reforms do not have large-firm creation as the objective.

Governments should also strive to ensure that private actors have the skills, technology, market intelligence, infrastructure, and finance they need to create large ventures. Reducing informational barriers that hinder the adoption of good managerial and production processes, improving access to technology, and providing incentives to adopt standards are particularly promising in fostering the growth of small and medium enterprises as a channel of large-firm creation. But this channel is unlikely to be sufficient in filling the "missing top" by itself. Across low- and middle-income countries, only 1 in 10 small firms grows to medium size, and only 1 in 100 grows to become a large firm. Complementing policies that foster small and medium enterprise development with policies that foster large-firm creation from other sources—foreign direct investment through investment promotion and spinoffs of other large firms—is also necessary.

Finally, governments and development finance institutions (DFIs) should actively work to spread the benefits from production at scale across the largest possible number of market participants. Large firms create demand in their supply chains, grow markets of previously unavailable products and services, generate surpluses that can improve workers' income and employment conditions, and generate know-how in ways that benefit other companies of all sizes. Governments and DFIs have an important role to play for these effects to materialize: taking a value chain perspective and partnering with larger firms—both incumbent firms and new challengers—in each industry to train, connect, and improve the functioning of product and labor markets is necessary to allow other participants to benefit from their growth. In the future, technological change could erode some of the benefits that come with production at scale, while increasing others. Market contestability should be the guiding pillar for large-firm creation—it will enable markets to adapt and work for the largest possible number of participants.

Note on COVID-19

The analysis and recommendations of this book were prepared before the COVID-19 outbreak. Since the pandemic began in 2020, the global economy has suffered the most severe shock since World War II, affecting firms of all sizes and their contributions to the livelihoods of the poor. A disorderly exit of otherwise viable firms in this context would set back the process of structural transformation and progress toward inclusive growth. It can create lasting effects on productivity, employment, and competition. That risk warrants temporary and transparent government support for vulnerable private firms targeted to the extent possible toward growth-oriented enterprises and competitive sectors suffering the greatest loss of capital.

The findings of this study are even more relevant in this context. Productive large firms can play a key role in restoring growth and creating jobs in the aftermath of the pandemic, so recovery plans should include actions to promote large-scale entrepreneurship and foreign direct investment. Strengthening firm capabilities to adapt and grow in an era of rapidly changing markets should be an immediate priority, in addition to liquidity support. Open and contestable markets will be critical for a faster recovery.

12 Empirical Highlights

1. Across 9 low- and middle-income countries with available business census data, nearly **6 out of 10** large enterprises are also the most productive in their country and sector. In services, the overlap drops to fewer than **2 out of 10** large firms.

2. A large foreign-owned firm is **25 percent** more likely than its large domestic competitors to be among the most productive firms in its country and sector. A large state-owned enterprise, by contrast, is **three times** less likely to be among the most productive firms in its country and sector.

3. Workers in large firms report **22 percent** higher hourly wages, on average, in a pooled sample of household and labor surveys from 32 low- and middle-income countries. Accounting for worker characteristics and nonpecuniary benefits, the large-firm wage premium remains close to **15 percent** on average. The magnitude of the premium is significantly higher in lower-income contexts.

4. Large firms account for **more than half** of aggregate net job creation across 6 countries for which we have both an industrial census and official statistics on employment growth. These contributions are generally higher in manufacturing than in services.

5. The employment share of 300+ employee firms is nearly **5 percentage points** lower, on average, than the share predicted by a Pareto distribution in a sample of 6 low- and middle-income countries with available business census data. In Indonesia, the lower share of labor in larger manufacturing firms corresponds to more than **230,000 jobs**.

6. Of all firms that enter with fewer than 20 employees and survive for at least five years across our sample of countries, nearly **9 out of 10** are still small by the end of five years. Only **1 in 10** grows to become a medium-size firm, and **1 in 100** grows to become a large firm.

7. Nearly **half** of large establishments surveyed by the World Bank in low-income countries were already large when they started operating. The share drops to **one-third** in middle-income economies and to **less than 30 percent** in high-income countries.

8. Among managers of large firms appraised by the International Finance Corporation, **98 percent** have other experience in the same sector of economic activity. Of those who also have experience in a sector other than the one in which the firm is operating, more than **40 percent** have experience in finance.

9. Firms that start large are at least **two times** more likely than the rest to export at origin and **three to four times** more likely to report multiple-sector activities.

10. Both firms that grow large from smaller sizes, and those that start off large, pay between **25 and 50 percent** higher wages than the rest at origin and report, on average, **1** additional employment layer at origin.

11. Regulatory protection of incumbents in upper-middle-income and lower-middle-income countries is more than **40 percent** and **60 percent** greater, on average, than the level observed in high-income countries.

12. A large firm is **5 to 10 percent more** likely to report customs operations, the court system, workforce skills, transportation, and telecommunications infrastructure as constraining its operations; **3 to 7 percent less** likely to report the availability of finance as a constraint; and **9 to 12 percent less** likely to report competition from the informal sector as a constraint.

Abbreviations

FDI	foreign direct investment
GDP	gross domestic product
IFC	International Finance Corporation
OECD	Organisation for Economic Co-operation and Development
PPP	public-private partnership
SMEs	small and medium enterprises

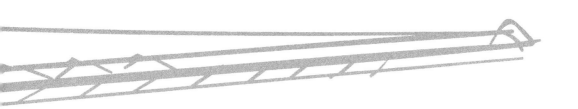

Introduction

Firms do not all serve the same purpose

Scale is a fundamental element of economic activity. As production is reorganized from individuals to firms and from smaller to larger firms, resources are better used, firms take advantage of economies of scale and scope, and they invest in innovation, standards, and human capital. Scale is ultimately associated with productivity, which is a driving force of growth.

Yet firms do not all serve the same purpose in organized markets and societies. While scale improves efficiency and returns for the market as a whole, smaller firms ensure that economic activity occurs in a greater variety of essential services, across densely populated but also remote locations, and for less dynamic segments of society for which business is a way of making a living. Economic and social progress requires a diverse ecosystem of firms serving multiple objectives in parallel.

The availability of a variety of products and services in an economy is intrinsically associated with size diversity across firms undertaking different activities. Minimum efficient scale—that is, the minimum size at which a firm can sustain operations without making losses—depends on the cost of establishing production in different industries. In the telecommunications industry, for example, that minimum scale is large, because the fixed cost of establishing service provision is large. In the retail industry, by contrast, the fixed cost is small and so is the minimum efficient scale. Essential services—such as construction, business services, or personal care—are typically provided at smaller scale, customized to client needs. The welfare of societies and healthy market ecosystems depend on these activities.

Size diversity is also needed to ensure that business occurs across a wide range of locations. Scale involves the concentration of production in space, which greatly accelerated during the waves of industrial revolutions, when goods started moving inexpensively and rapidly across locations. While trade and transport infrastructure ensure access to goods in remote locations, access to services requires proximity. Universal service provision is thus dependent on smaller firms that can operate in remote locations.

Economic activity, finally, does not serve the same purpose for everyone. For the majority of entrepreneurs in low- and middle-income countries for which we have evidence, an enterprise is a way of making a living (Schoar 2010). Businesses that are less motivated by growth tend to remain small, not necessarily because of inefficiencies they cannot overcome, but because of the less ambitious plans of their owners and sponsors faced with a scarcity of wage employment. The purpose they serve is no less legitimate than the ambition of their growing competitors. Improving their returns and the sustainability of their operations can be an equally important policy objective that is aligned with the principle of leaving no one behind.

This report argues that large firms advance a range of economic and social objectives in ways that other firms do not. While these objectives are critical to development, the contribution of large firms remains part of an aggregate that is not served exclusively by large firms. The fact that lower-income countries lack large firms is a handicap for an ecosystem of firms, constraining the growth and survival of smaller enterprises and, ultimately, the growth and survival of healthy markets that work for all.

How large is large?

Economic theory does not provide clear guidance on what constitutes a large firm. At the edges of the firm-size distribution, there is little ambiguity in this respect: a 10,000-employee firm is universally considered large, and a 10-employee firm is considered small. But where in between should one draw the line? Is there an objective market or sector measure that puts a firm's size in perspective?

The question of how large is large is not only of academic interest. When designing industrial or innovation policies, governments often target growth of firms of a specific size (small or medium) or potential (high growth), which requires a clearly defined selection criterion. By exclusion, any criterion used for targeting small and medium enterprises (SMEs) implicitly defines a threshold above which firms are considered to be large.

FIGURE I.1   The regulatory cutoff for "large" varies by economy, by employment

American Samoa	Albania				Korea, Rep. Vietnam		Canada
					IFC		
Burkina Faso	AfDB	World Bank	Australia	EU			Canada
	Belize	Bangladesh	Colombia	IDB			United States
	Bolivia	Botswana	Egypt, Arab Rep.	UNDP			Yemen, Rep.
	Guam	Brunei Darussalam	Israel	Algeria			
	Jamaica	Cambodia	Morocco	Bahrain			
	Kenya	Costa Rica	Mozambique	Belarus			
	Lebanon	Domenican Republic	Nigeria	Bosnia and Herzegovina			
	Trinidad and Tobago	El Salvador	Philippines	Brazil			
		Georgia	Saudi Arabia	Kazakhstan			
		Ghana	Singapore	Mexico			
		Honduras	Tajikistan	Moldova			
		Hong Kong SAR, China	Thailand	Montenegro			
		Indonesia		North Macedonia			
		Japan		Norway			
		Jordan		Pakistan			
		Kyrgyz Republic		Puerto Rico			
		Lao PDR		Russian Federation			
		Malawi		Serbia			
		New Zealand		Switzerland			
		Nicaragua		Turkey			
		Oman		Uganda			
		Peru		Ukraine			
		Rwanda					
		Tanzania					
		Uruguay					
		Venezuela, RB					

Source: IFC and SME Business Forum 2017.
Note: AfDB = African Development Bank. IDB = Inter-American Development Bank. IFC = International Finance Corporation. UNDP = United Nations Development Programme.

The most commonly used criterion is employment—that is, the total number of people employed by the firm. Figure I.1 presents cutoffs that various jurisdictions and international organizations use to define SMEs and, by extension, large firms. Although 100 is the most popular choice, the cutoffs vary substantially across countries, from below 50 in some small economies such as Burkina Faso to 500 in large countries such as Canada.[1] International organizations do not have a consistent threshold either; the European Union uses a threshold of 250+, while the World Bank uses thresholds of 100+ and 300+ for its private sector development arm, the International Finance Corporation (IFC).

Larger jurisdictions tend to add nuance by applying different thresholds by industry, taking into account the minimum efficient scale and average size of firms relative to their competitors. Mixed systems exist for defining size as well, with some using not only employment but also revenue or total assets. The United States Small Business Administration also applies thresholds that vary by industry—larger for manufacturing, lower for services. The European Union, however, applies a generic threshold of 250 employees or €50 million in sales to all industries, implying that many firms considered large in Europe may be considered medium in the United States.

Having a generic threshold may reflect a desire on the part of policy makers to include a greater share of workers with benefits from SME programs. In the United States, the share of employment in SMEs defined according to the official threshold is 52 percent, but in Germany it is 63 percent and in Portugal it is 78 percent (OECD 2017; United States Census Bureau 2018). In India, a lower-middle-income country, the threshold of what is large is scaled down to fit the economy; a firm is considered large if it has investment in plants and machinery worth more than US$700,000, a criterion that would apply to most manufacturing firms in the United States.

Governments also make judgments about what is large when choosing whether to enforce certain regulations—for example, related to labor and taxes. These thresholds exist typically because it would be too costly to enforce regulations below that scale. They also tend to be lower than thresholds defined by SME programs (Garicano, LeLarge, and Van Reenen 2013). For instance, in France and the United States, certain regulations determine eligibility using the threshold of 50 employees, far below the thresholds used to define SMEs in those markets.

Ultimately, the conventions used to define "large" depend on the purpose and perceptions of different market actors. They often reflect an underlying economic rationale in their nuances across industries and the use of criteria—a rationale that is challenging to measure with precision and often can only be approximated. However, they have largely remained conventions. The critical question becomes whether these definitions still ensure selectivity—that is, whether they capture a group that is dissimilar from the average firm in quantitative and qualitative terms.

Adopting a rather conservative definition of large firm—the most widely used threshold of 100 employees—fulfills that objective. However generic, the threshold consistently captures a leading minority of firms: fewer than 1 out of 20 formal enterprises in low- and middle-income countries but also high- income countries operate at that scale (see figure I.2 on firm size distributions in manufacturing and services for Spain and Vietnam as two illustrative cases). These firms also make disproportionally high contributions to employment. Despite accounting for less than 5 percent of the total number of manufacturing firms, firms with 100+ employees employ, for instance, about 40 percent of total number of manufacturing workers in Spain and 80 percent in Vietnam. The same holds for many other countries independent of their level of development.

There is value in showing that firms at this conservative threshold are different—it makes our insights applicable to many more cases and presents a workable and manageable target for both governments and development institutions. Throughout this report, we use a generic threshold of 100 employees to define large firms, highlighting at all stages what is different about the larger firms within that segment (that is, those with 300+ and 500+ employees).

In the rest of this report, we address four questions in detail. First, *how are large firms different from the rest of firms in low- and middle-income countries?* We delve into the distinct features of large firms that work for

FIGURE I.2   Firm-size distribution and employment shares: Vietnam and Spain, 2012

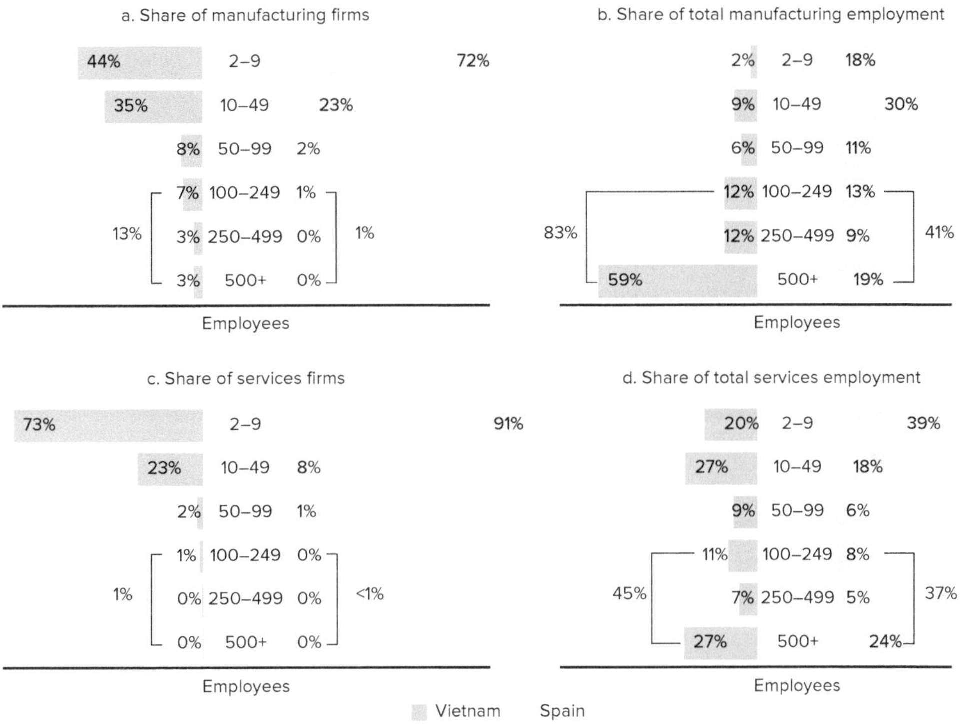

a. Share of manufacturing firms

44%	2–9	72%
35%	10–49	23%
8%	50–99	2%
7%	100–249	1%
13% 3%	250–499	0% 1%
3%	500+	0%

Employees

b. Share of total manufacturing employment

2%	2–9	18%
9%	10–49	30%
6%	50–99	11%
12%	100–249	13%
83% 12%	250–499	9% 41%
59%	500+	19%

Employees

c. Share of services firms

73%	2–9	91%
23%	10–49	8%
2%	50–99	1%
1%	100–249	0%
1% 0%	250–499	0% <1%
0%	500+	0%

Employees

d. Share of total services employment

20%	2–9	39%
27%	10–49	18%
9%	50–99	6%
11%	100–249	8%
45% 7%	250–499	5% 37%
27%	500+	24%

Employees

☐ Vietnam   Spain

Sources: For Vietnam, business census data (2012); for Spain, Organisation for Economic Co-operation and Development (OECD) DynEmp data.

development—such as income generation, job creation, and innovation—and explore their fundamental links with productivity and market contestability. These firm-level differences translate into better aggregate outcomes, making firms vehicles of change. But *is there a shortage of large, firms in low- and middle-income countries?* The frequency with which we encounter large, productive firms in low- and middle-income countries represents the core of the problem: it is significantly lower than expected. So, *where do new large firms come from?* Who creates them, how do they look at the beginning, and what are the circumstances of their creation? Few scholars have examined these questions because of the scarcity of evidence. We describe sources of large-firm creation—such as entrepreneurship, foreign investment, spin-offs from other large firms, and governments—and we track the growth paths of large firms during the first years of their operations to illustrate attributes and strategies that bring them to scale. The evidence invites a forward-looking final question: *how do we fill the gap?* With market contestability serving as a guide, we explore solutions that could work for large-firm creation in lower-income contexts and the role of development finance in the process.

Note

1 | According to micro, small, and medium enterprise country indicators. For more information, see IFC and SME Business Forum (2017).

References

Garicano, Luis, Claire LeLarge, and John Van Reenen. 2013. "Firm Size Distortions and the Productivity Distribution: Evidence from France." NBER Working Paper 18841, National Bureau of Economic Research, Cambridge, MA.

IFC (International Finance Corporation) and SME (Small and Medium Enterprise) Business Forum. 2017. MSME Country Indicators database. Washington, DC: IFC. https://www.smefinanceforum.org /data-sites/msme-country-indicators.

OECD (Organisation for Economic Co-operation and Development). 2017. *Entrepreneurship at a Glance*. Paris: OECD Publishing. https://www.oecd-ilibrary.org/employment/entrepreneurship-at-a -glance-2017/employment-by-enterprise-size_entrepreneur_aag-2017-6-en.

OECD (Organisation for Economic Co-operation and Development). Various years. DynEmp (Measuring Job Creation by Start-ups and Young Firms) database. Paris: OECD, Directorate for Science, Technology, and Innovation. http://www.oecd.org/sti/dynemp.htm.

Schoar, Antoinette. 2010. "The Divide between Subsistence and Transformational Entrepreneurship." In *Innovation Policy and the Economy,* vol. 10, edited by Josh Lerner and Scott Stern, 57–81. Chicago: University of Chicago Press.

United States Census Bureau. 2018. SUSB (Statistics of United States Businesses) database. Washington, DC: United States Census Bureau. https://www.census.gov/programs-surveys/susb.html.

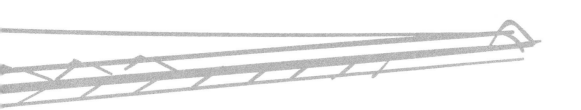

1. Large firms make distinct contributions to development

Large firms in low- and middle-income countries have several features that set them apart from smaller competitors. This chapter systematically examines the distinct features that are closely associated with their productivity advantages over smaller firms—that is, their ability to lower the costs of production through economies of scale and scope but also to invest in quality and access demand. Large firms frequently pursue better management and organization of production, as well as seeking outward orientation, innovation, and investment in human capital. This translates into better outcomes for their owners, and also for their workers and for smaller enterprises in their value chains. Large firms ultimately represent vehicles of change, driving a substantial share of aggregate economic activity in low- and middle-income countries, while contributing to net job creation and labor productivity growth across different contexts.

Yet this array of benefits does not come automatically with firm size. Market contestability (that is, whether more productive entrants can challenge the position of large incumbents) as well as the objectives of owners (whether they are foreign investors, domestic entrepreneurs, or government) to a large extent explain the strength of the association between scale and productivity advantages that ultimately drives better development outcomes.

The World Bank Enterprise Surveys are a unique source of information for studying these questions; the set used in the analysis contains detailed information about more than 70,000 establishments in 123 economies.[1] Industrial censuses from 10 low- and middle-income countries offer additional insights, as do other microdata sets, such as the International Income Distribution Data Set (I2D2)—the largest set of globally harmonized household and labor survey data collected by the World Bank, which provides a closer look at the quality of jobs provided by large firms—and the Organisation for Economic Co-operation and Development's (OECD) Orbis and DynEmp databases, which include millions of observations from firms in high-income countries, illustrating how large firms in industrial markets differ with respect to their peers in less developed economies.

Firm size is associated with productivity

Firm size is associated with productivity—that is, the effective transformation of inputs into output and returns. Scale and productivity can reinforce each other in a virtuous cycle. Large firms benefit from economies of scale to lower the costs of production or service provision: the more a firm produces, the lower the average cost incurred per unit, because the fixed costs are spread over a larger amount of output. Often, a single large firm is able to produce a bundle of several goods and services more cheaply than a group of more specialized enterprises—a concept known as "economies of scope." Larger firms also have margins to invest in quality and to access greater demand, both of which boost returns. Lower costs of production, better quality, and higher demand, in turn, enable firms to grow even larger.

Theory offers insights into factors that underlie the productivity selection driving firm growth at the beginning of the virtuous cycle. Lucas's influential model of firm size, for example, predicts that average firm size is driven by "managerial talent" that generates more output from the available capital per worker (Lucas 1978). Although entrepreneurs face decreasing returns to capital and labor, use of this multiplier gives some firms a larger optimal scale than others. The organization of production along the value chain also matters (Grossman and Hart 1986). Firms become larger when it is more efficient to make a product internally than to outsource it or buy it from the market. Ownership, market intelligence, and many competitive advantages can be added to this list.

A close empirical association between scale and productivity is common in the literature. In both high-income and low- and middle-income economies, large firms tend to have higher total factor productivity and higher rates of productivity growth (Ayyagari, Demirgüç-Kunt, and Maksimovic 2014; Haltiwanger, Jarmin, and Miranda 2013; Leung, Meh, and Terajima 2008; Poschke 2018). A glance at firm-level industrial census data from nine countries—China, Côte d'Ivoire, Ethiopia, Indonesia, Kosovo, Morocco, Moldova, Serbia, and Vietnam—confirms a significant overlap between scale and productivity (figure 1.1; see chapter 3 for a description of the data). Distinguishing between (a) large firms with more than 100 employees and (b) the same number of most productive firms within each country, sector, and year yields an overlap of nearly 60 percent. In other words, nearly 6 out of 10 large enterprises are also the most productive in the same country and sector.[2] More formally, doubling firm employment is associated with an average 9 percent increase in value added per employee, taking into account country, sector, and year differences.

Yet size does not reflect productivity in every sector and context. While in manufacturing the overlap is more than 60 percent, in services fewer than 2 out of 10 large firms are also the most productive in their sector (figure 1.1). Minimum efficient scale is one natural explanation for some of this variation. In the tele-communications industry, for example, the minimum scale above which a firm can operate without losses is large because the fixed cost of establishing service provision is high. Larger firms in that sector may not necessarily be the most productive ones. In the retail industry, by contrast, the fixed cost is small and so is the minimum efficient scale.

Market contestability—that is, the ease with which entrants can challenge the position of large incumbents—could also explain much of the discrepancy. Contestability is difficult to measure. It refers to the level of competition, but also the ease of entry, the threat of entry, the ability of new entrants to compete, and a range of correlated factors that force firms to be more productive and to share a greater portion of their returns to maintain operations. The sector of economic activity—manufacturing or services—is a rough but good predictor of the aggregate of these factors. The few studies that have attempted to esti-mate competitive pressure beyond manufacturing have found systematically less competition in services (Bottini and Molnar 2010; Bouis and Klein 2008; Christopoulou and Vermeulen 2008; Høj et al. 2007). There is no single expla-nation for this finding. Customization and the difficulty of realizing economies of scale could explain lower contestability in some services—for example, legal or accounting services—while the opposite could be true for network indus-tries, such as telecommunications, where high fixed costs of entry are the main source of market power and where state intervention often constrains competition.

More generally, competition in services is often based on quality and diversification rather than cost efficiency, both of which offer protection against competitive pressures (Antoniades 2015). A corollary of this feature is a loose(r) association between scale and productivity in services: large service providers are often able to capture high demand in narrow uncontested segments. Of greater significance is the hypothesis that an economy's diversification into services in the course of its development could weaken the association between scale and productivity, which could erode some of the benefits of large firms.

FIGURE 1.1 Venn diagrams: Overlap between large and more productive firms

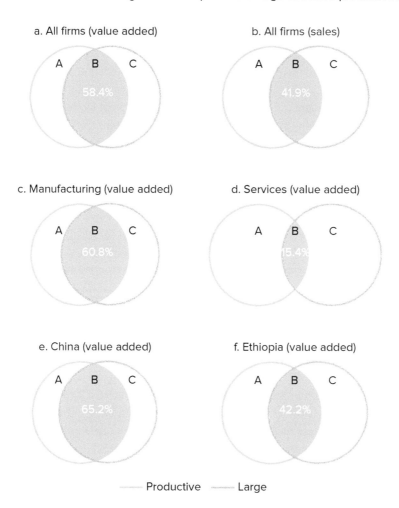

a. All firms (value added)

b. All firms (sales)

c. Manufacturing (value added)

d. Services (value added)

e. China (value added)

f. Ethiopia (value added)

———— Productive ———— Large

Source: Calculations based on industrial census data from a selection of countries.
Note: Firm productivity is calculated as the moving three-year average of firm value added or sales per employee using constant US$. Employment refers to total number of employees. A = small and productive firms (total employment < 100 and within the higher-productivity segment). B = large and productive firms (total employment ≥ 100 and within the higher-productivity segment). C = large and unproductive firms.

Cross-country variation in the link between scale and productivity is also considerable, even within manufacturing. In China, for example, across all sectors, the relationship between scale and productivity is tighter than in the rest of the sample, whereas overlap is estimated at the lower levels of 32 percent in Côte d'Ivoire, 42 percent in Ethiopia, 10 percent in Moldova, and 14 percent in Serbia. This variation suggests that market size as well as, potentially, the history of industrial development and features of the business environment beyond contestability all affect the strength of association between scale and productivity.

Ownership matters

Whether productivity serves the main objective function of the firm is reflected in its relationship with scale. We find that a large state-owned enterprise is three times less likely to be in the upper productivity segment of the same sector and year than a privately owned large firm. Excluding state-owned enterprises, the overlap between scale and productivity in all firms rises to more than 60 percent. By contrast, a foreign-owned large firm is 25 percent more likely than a domestic private firm to be in the upper productivity segment and multiple times more likely than a firm in the lower segment (figure 1.2).

These results are not surprising. State-owned enterprises deviate from the average private firm in many respects: they are less profitable, more labor intensive, and heavily leveraged; they also have easier access to credit than private firms (Boycko, Shleifer, and Vishny 1996; DeWenter and Malatesta 2001;

FIGURE 1.2   Probability that a firm belongs to a particular segment

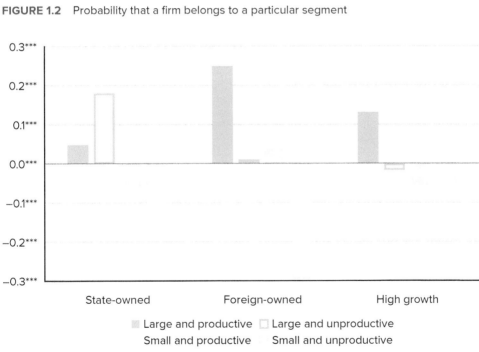

Source: Calculations based on industrial census data from a selection of countries.
Note: The probability that a firm belongs to each of the four segments is calculated using four linear ordinary least squares regressions $G_{it} = S_{it} + F_{it} + H_{it} + k + s + t + \varepsilon_{it}$; k, s, t, are country sector and year fixed effects respectively, where G_{it} is a binary indicator of whether the firm is classified as small and productive, large and productive, large and unproductive, small and unproductive in year t, respectively, as defined in figure 1.1. S_{it} and F_{it} are binary indicators of state and foreign ownership, respectively, and H_{it} is an indicator of high employment growth, as defined in Eurostat and OECD (2007). The bars on the chart indicate the level of the coefficients on the regressors S_{it}, F_{it}, and H_{it} in each of the four regressions.
*** All coefficients reported in this figure are significant at the 1% level.

Liu, Tian, and Wang 2011). Their underperformance is often due to the mix of social and commercial objectives they pursue, to poor performance monitoring, and to their regulatory protection from competition. Governments' willingness to make up for their commercial losses heavily distorts incentives and leads to low productivity. Foreign ownership, by contrast, is associated with several advantages that enhance productivity, such as possession of more advanced technology, managerial know-how, and access to foreign demand.

How much more productive are large firms?

The World Bank Enterprise Surveys offer unique data for exploring this question across countries for different measures of efficiency; labor productivity (sales per worker), total factor productivity (the part of production output not explained by inputs of capital and labor), capacity utilization, growth of sales, and growth of employment all reflect competitive performance.

The differences between the estimates coming from the World Bank Enterprise Surveys and the business censuses may reflect their coverage

---

BOX 1.1   Comparability of data on establishments versus firms

The World Bank Enterprise Surveys are establishment-level surveys from 144 countries that have been collected using a standard methodology since 2006. Other data sets used to examine business dynamics, such as business censuses or commercially available databases, are reported at the level of firms. How comparable is the evidence collected at the level of establishments, firms, business groups, value chains, or conglomerates?

There are advantages and disadvantages to using establishments as the unit of observation. To the extent that we are interested in the scale of firms, and large-firm premiums in particular, large firms that operate many small establishments will be misclassified. The potentially superior performance of these small establishments, which can be explained partly by the fact that they operate as units of a large enterprise, may shrink differences along the size distribution and may downward-bias large-firm premiums. The World Bank Enterprise Surveys alleviate this potential bias by collecting information on whether an establishment is part of a multiple-establishment firm.

However, large enterprises often tend to be active in multiple business sectors, which they report at the level of establishments, keeping only the record of the main activity at the level of the enterprise. Netting out the effects of sectors in a regression framework would be more accurate at the level of establishments, even when firms are the ultimate unit of interest. The same holds for the effects of geographic location on the firm's performance.

The biases introduced as the level of analysis moves from establishments to firms also apply as the analysis moves to higher levels of aggregation. Firms that belong to business conglomerates, for example, enjoy premiums that are not captured accurately by restricting the level of analysis to the firm. Ultimately, to the extent that we are interested in analyzing scale of production as an outcome or driver of business behavior, results at all levels of analysis would be relevant, with the caveat that if we find significant differences between large and small firms, these differences are likely to vary as we change the main unit of observation.

FIGURE 1.3 Large-firm premiums on selected indicators of performance

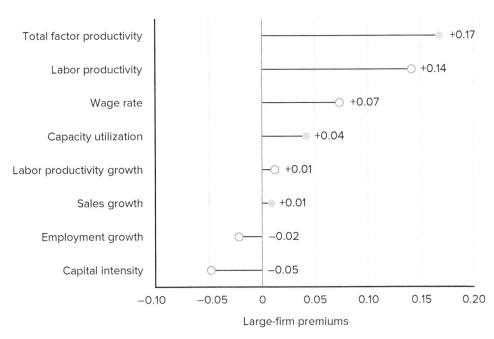

○ Premium with lower statistical significance once other firm characteristics are accounted for

Source: Calculations based on World Bank Enterprise Survey data (2018).
Note: This figure presents the coefficient on the large firm binary variable in a series of linear ordinary least square regressions with each performance indicator as a dependent variable, and controls for country and sector fixed effects.

(box 1.1). On the one hand, there are fewer larger firms among large firms in each country, potentially because the surveys are less likely to sample firms in the thin but long right-side tail of the size distribution. On the other hand, there is a much greater variety of contexts—123 countries included in the analysis— and, in many of them, large firms may operate in less contestable markets and deliver less on their potential.

The evidence highlights advantages of large establishments relative to smaller ones in most of these measures of performance (see figure 1.3). We refer to these differences as "large-firm premiums," bearing in mind the distinctions of establishment-level and firm-level analysis (see appendix A for details of the methodology).[3] First, large firms have, on average, higher levels of labor productivity, which appear to be driven entirely by their capital intensity. Once the amount of capital that firms use in production is taken into account, the premium disappears. Put differently, higher sales per worker for large firms relative to small and medium enterprises (SMEs) seem to be driven entirely by large firms' use of more capital in the production process.[4]

In addition, the evidence confirms that large firms are better able than SMEs to combine labor and capital and to achieve higher total factor productivity. This relationship remains strong and sizable, even after accounting for other firm characteristics, such as age, foreign ownership, and exporting status. Large firms are also better able to mobilize their resources, achieving higher capacity utilization. This evidence indicates that large firms produce output at levels closer to their maximum potential. Large firms also have higher levels of sales growth, but not employment or labor productivity growth, relative to SMEs.

The larger among large firms perform better in some dimensions

A relatively conservative definition of large firms (that is, firms with 100 or more employees) conceals important variations within the large-firm segment of the firm-size distribution. The source of this variation is fairly intuitive: the larger among large firms may be substantively different in their operations and may contribute substantially more in quantitative terms to aggregate outcomes. Uneven qualitative contributions are also expected, given that certain strategies, such as outward orientation, may be more successful for the larger ones among large firms.

The evidence confirms this intuition: establishments with 300 or more employees—ones that are at least three times larger than the definition of large firms given above—use their capital better, are considerably more likely to export, offer training more frequently, have greater access to external finance, and have significantly higher adoption rates for international standards than SMEs (figure 1.4).

Whether doubling a firm's size would lead to a proportionate increase in its contribution to aggregate outcomes remains an open question. Estimates of returns to scale have not produced consistent results, with wide variation observed across countries and industries. While the World Bank Enterprise Surveys provide evidence that some benefits increase with firm size, as expected, the evidence on the exact factor of returns is weak.

Size is a proxy for a package of characteristics and strategies

The close association between firm size and productivity is reflected in a variety of other firm characteristics—such as age, ownership, managerial ability,

FIGURE 1.4   Large-firm premium differences between 100+ and 300+ firms on selected indicators

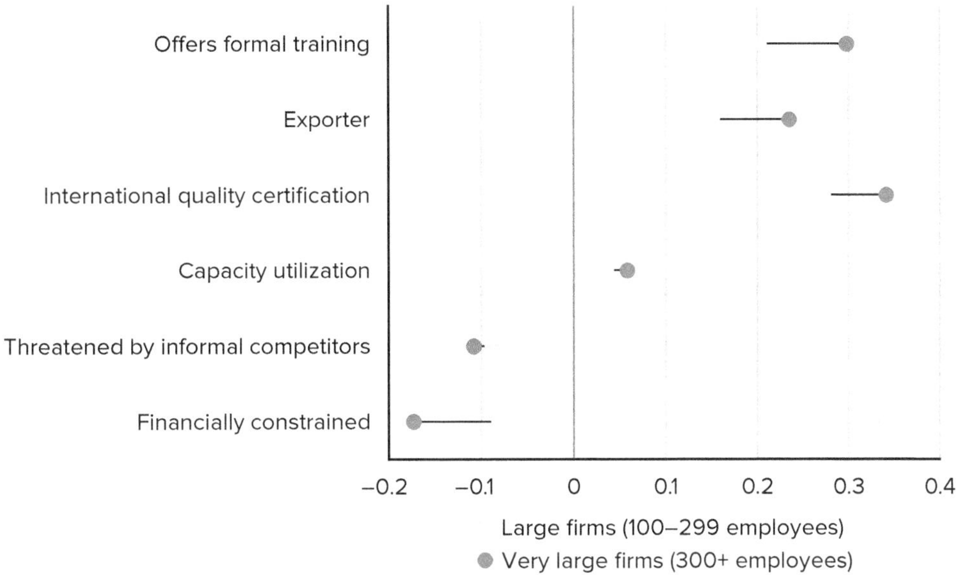

Large firms (100–299 employees)
● Very large firms (300+ employees)

Source: Calculations based on World Bank Enterprise Survey data (2018).
Note: This figure presents the coefficients on two large firm binary variables for 100+ and 300+ definitions, in linear ordinary least square regressions with each outcome indicator as a dependent variable, controlling for country and sector fixed effects.

outward orientation, and innovation—which are likely to drive and be driven by scale. Evidence confirms the close association between these features, all of which can be proxied by scale.

Age

Age is the characteristic that is associated perhaps most visibly and intuitively with firm size. The larger a firm is when it starts up, or the larger it grows, the more likely it is to survive; the average age of large firms surveyed by the World Bank in low- and middle-income countries is about 20 years, 5 years above the average age of smaller firms (figure 1.5).[5] This finding is consistent with the existing literature. Although data sets containing information about firms' age are rather rare (most administrative data lack this information) (Headd and Kirchhoff 2009), studies that explore both size and age find that large firms are generally considerably older than SMEs (Ayyagari, Demirgüç-Kunt, and Maksimovic 2011; Criscuolo, Gal, and Menon 2014; Haltiwanger, Jarmin, and Miranda 2013).

Because firms' age and size are closely associated, distinguishing the effect of each on firms' outcomes is more meaningful. In fact, the two have often been confounded in studies of firm size and its effects; various firm outcomes have long been attributed to their size rather than their age (Anyadike-Danes et al. 2015; Ayyagari, Demirgüç-Kunt, and Maksimovic 2014; Criscuolo, Gal, and Menon 2014; Haltiwanger, Jarmin, and Miranda 2013). For example, it has long been believed that larger firms grow less (on net), although this relationship disappears once firm age is taken into account (Haltiwanger, Jarmin, and Miranda 2013).

FIGURE 1.5   Age distribution of firms, by size and country income group

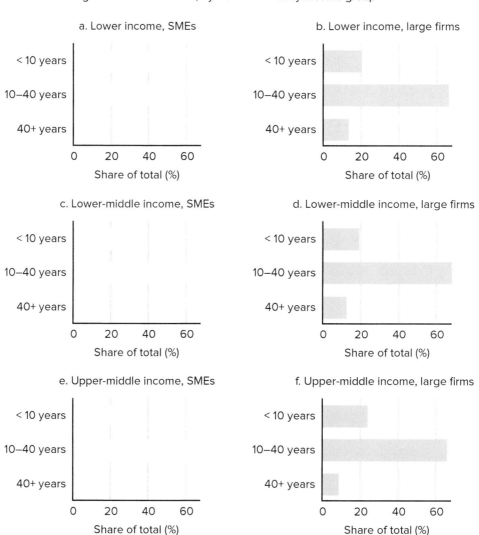

Source: Calculations based on World Bank Enterprise Survey data (2018).
Note: SMEs = small and medium enterprises.

Ownership dispersion and management

A concentrated ownership structure is less likely in larger firms. This relation may be suggestive of adjustments to varying levels of risk, leading individuals to diversify more as the stakes rise (Demsetz and Lehn 1985). The World Bank Enterprise Survey data suggest that large firms are considerably less likely than SMEs to have ownership concentrated in the hands of a single person or to have a legal form of sole proprietorship.

Evidence also confirms another intuitive association: that, perhaps as part of better access to higher-quality human capital in general, large firms employ more experienced managers—in particular, ones with longer experience of working in the relevant sector. This rather sizable discrepancy in managerial quality is also evident in the considerable difference in the management practices of large firms compared with those of SMEs (see box 1.2 for more detail for a subset of countries where the World Bank Enterprise Surveys collected additional information about firms' management practices).

Outward orientation

Moving beyond firms' age and managerial ability, many features set large firms apart. An important example of this is firms' exporting status—in other words, firms' ability to access demand. Participating in exports is often considered a "hallmark of productivity," achieved only by high-performing firms (Ter Wengel and Rodriguez 2006, 25). This view is justified, given that exporting activity is positively and robustly related to other indicators of

---

BOX 1.2   Size and management practices in Latin America and the Caribbean

The effects of firms' management practices on their performance are a relatively new and important avenue of investigation (Bloom et al. 2012, 2013). The ways in which firms are managed appear to differ substantially across firms and countries. Moreover, the evidence that management practices are closely related to firms' performance and high-growth episodes is accumulating quickly (for example, Goswami, Medvedev, and Olafsen 2019).

To quantify the role of management practices, Bloom and Van Reenen (2007) developed a set of survey questions, which was adopted by the United States Census Bureau and implemented as the Management and Organizational Practices Survey (MOPS) in 2010—the first large-scale survey on the topic. Based on MOPS and in collaboration with Bloom and Van Reenen (2007, 2010), the World Bank Enterprise Surveys modified these questions and implemented them as part of standard Enterprise Surveys. These questions have already been fielded in the most recent World Bank Enterprise Surveys in seven Latin American countries (Argentina, Bolivia, Colombia, Ecuador, Paraguay, Peru, and Uruguay).[a]

(continued)

BOX 1.2   *Continued*

FIGURE B1.2.1   Large-firm premiums on indicators of managerial practices

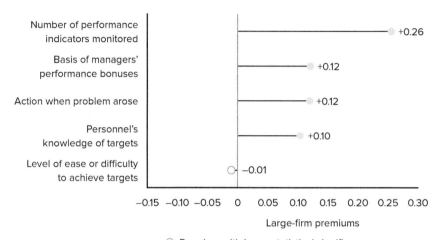

Source: Calculations based on World Bank Enterprise Survey data (2018).
Note: This figure presents the coefficient on the large firm binary variable in a series of linear ordinary least square regressions with each performance indicator as a dependent variable, and controls for country and sector fixed effects.

FIGURE B1.2.2   Average aggregate management score premium of large firms

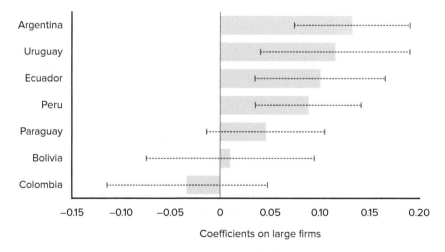

Source: Calculations based on World Bank Enterprise Survey data (2018).
Note: This figure presents the coefficient on the large firm binary variable in a linear ordinary least squares regression for each country with the aggregate management score as the dependent variable, and controls for firm characteristics and sector fixed effects. A 95% confidence interval is included in the figure.

(continued)

BOX 1.2 *Continued*

The surveys capture five components of management practices, which can be aggregated into a single score, with a higher score denoting "better" management practices. For example, the survey asks, "What action is taken when a problem arises in production?" The responses indicate less structured actions ("No action was taken") or more structured actions ("We fixed it and took action to make sure it did not happen again")—with a higher score assigned to the more structured practice. The data show that, in general, large firms have better-structured management practices. The only component where no large-firm premium exists relates to the level of difficulty of achieving targets for production or service provision. This finding could be due to firms of various sizes setting targets that match their abilities.

The average aggregate management practice score across all firms is 0.54, while for large firms it is 0.64, suggesting a sizable large-firm premium. Looking at the aggregate score of management practices for each country separately, large firms appear to apply better management practices than SMEs in Argentina, Ecuador, Peru, and Uruguay; and this relationship holds even after accounting for country and sector of operation as well as firm characteristics. In Bolivia, Colombia, and Paraguay, once firm characteristics are accounted for, large firms do not differ from SMEs in their management practices.

a. Data from Argentina are included in the analysis for this box, but are excluded from the rest of the chapter. This is because the World Bank classified Argentina as high income in 2017, when the World Bank Enterprise Survey was implemented there.

success, such as firms' productivity, capital intensity, higher wages, episodes of high growth, and survival (Alvarez and Lopez 2005; Andersen 1993; Autio, Sapienza, and Almeida 2000; Bernard et al. 2007; Carpenter and Fredrickson 2001; Dominguez and Sequeira 1993; Goswami, Medvedev, and Olafsen 2019; Javorcik 2004; McDougall and Oviatt 2000; Olney 2016; Park, Shin, and Kim 2010; Regis 2018; Sapienza et al. 2006; Yang, Chen, and Chuang 2004; Yasuda 2005; Zahra, Ireland, and Hitt 2000).

The evidence from Enterprise Surveys not only confirms that larger firms are more likely to enter export markets but also provides information on additional ways in which large firms may exhibit outward orientation. Looking at foreign ownership, the use of foreign inputs, and international quality accreditation, the Enterprise Surveys confirm that, across all measures, large firms display significantly higher levels of outward orientation, as illustrated in figure 1.6. Each of these effects remains significant after accounting for a range of firm characteristics, confirming the robustness of this relationship (see appendix A for more details on the relevant regressions).

Innovation and investment in assets and people

Similar to exporting status, innovation offers firms new opportunities for growth, while also requiring considerable resources and effort, which may not be

FIGURE 1.6 Large-firm premiums in indicators of outward orientation

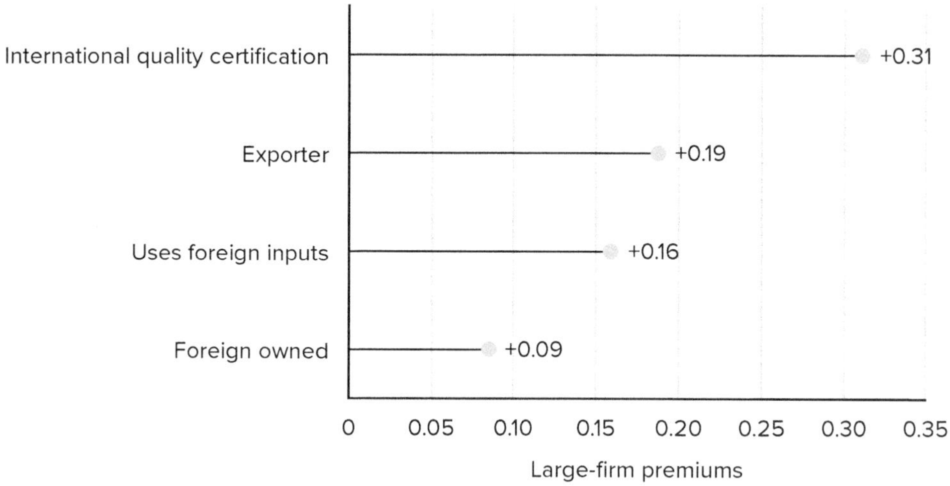

Source: Calculations based on World Bank Enterprise Survey data (2018).
Note: This figure presents the coefficient on large firm binary variable in a series of linear ordinary least square regressions with each performance indicator as a dependent variable, and controls for country and sector fixed effects.

affordable for all firms. Research and development (R&D) activities can be especially challenging for smaller firms because of the associated uncertainty, high fixed costs, and high level of minimum investments required, all coupled with hardship in accessing finance.

The relationship between firm size and the propensity to innovate or engage in R&D is corroborated in the Enterprise Survey data, as illustrated in figure 1.7. Innovation of various types is self-reported and time-bound in these surveys: owners or top managers of firms report whether they introduced a product, service, or process innovation within the last three years. Larger firms are more likely to have innovated and to report R&D spending, even after taking into account firm characteristics that are known to affect both firm size and innovation activities. The data allow us to distinguish innovations that are new not only to the firm itself but to its market. Using this more demanding measure of innovation, large firms are also more likely than SMEs to have introduced a product or process that is new to their market within the last three years (see appendix A figure A1.1 for additional results on innovation).

Apart from engaging in the process of developing and implementing innovations, firms may attempt to improve their performance by investing in their human and physical capital. Larger firms are likelier than SMEs to attract

FIGURE 1.7   Large-firm premiums in investment and innovation

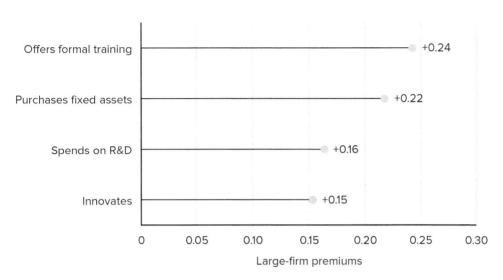

Source: Calculations based on World Bank Enterprise Survey data (2018).
Note: This figure presents the coefficient on the large firm binary variable in a series of linear ordinary least squares regressions with each outcome indicator as a dependent variable, and controls for country and sector fixed effects. R&D = research and development.

qualified labor (for example, Yang and Chen 2009), which may suggest less need to train workers. However, a higher rate of innovation by large firms may require more training of workers to implement these innovations. The Enterprise Survey data suggest the latter: larger firms are found to be considerably more likely to invest in their workers' training. Investments in physical capital—such as machinery, vehicles, equipment, land, and buildings—exhibit similar patterns across firms of different sizes. As figure 1.7 illustrates, there is a considerable large-firm premium in making such investments. Notably, this relationship also holds after taking into account firm characteristics that are known to be associated with investment behavior (such as age, export status, and foreign ownership), suggesting that size itself, perhaps together with other characteristics, underlies this premium.

Large-firm premiums might be different in high-income countries

Differences between large and smaller firms are not expected to be the same in countries at different levels of development. Distortions and market failures have an impact on the survival of different types of firms. In high-income countries, greater competition drives less productive firms—small or medium size—out of the market. Sharper distributions of firm productivity have been reported regularly in countries like Germany and the United States, where differences in productivity between larger and smaller firms shrink as smaller, less productive firms exit markets (EBRD 2018; World Bank 2012). Competitive distortions allow such firms to survive in lower-income countries, flattening the firm productivity distribution.

At the same time, the divergence between the global frontier and the rest of firms in high-income countries (Berlingieri, Blanchenay, and Criscuolo 2017) is expected to exacerbate rather than shrink gaps between large and smaller firms, possibly outweighing the effect of the exit of the latter on dissimilarities along the size distribution. In fact, estimates of large-firm premiums in four high-income countries—France, Italy, Spain, and Sweden—using the OECD's DynEmp and Orbis data yield significantly more pronounced differences between large and smaller firms than those observed in low- and middle-income countries (see appendix B for a description of the database). The gap between large and smaller firms in labor productivity is as much as four times greater, on average, in high-income countries, with differences in total factor productivity in manufacturing rising to six times; and differences in average wage and productivity growth are as much as four times greater as well (appendix B, figure B.1).

Although these gaps are consistent with the expected impact of frontier firms on dissimilarities along the firm-size distribution, the two samples used to measure them are not fully comparable, as suggested by a robustness test focusing on seven countries in Eastern and Central Europe and the year in which the two databases overlap (appendix B, figure B.1, right panel). Further work is needed to assess systematic differences between large and smaller firms in high-income markets relative to what is reported. Future Enterprise Surveys conducted in Western Europe will allow a more systematic comparison between the two databases using a consistent methodology.

Scale is associated with different returns to workers

Large firms pay higher wages. Moore (1911) first observed this regularity in an early-twentieth-century study of Italian textile mills, and subsequent analyses have established it as a stylized fact of the labor market globally (Barth, Davis, and Freeman 2018; Bayard and Troske 1999; Brown and Medoff 1989; Fafchamps and Söderbom 2006; Mazumdar and Mazaheri 2002; Oi and Idson 1999; Troske 1999; Velenchik 1997).

Better returns to labor are associated with better returns to capital and firm productivity. This association is confirmed across the board in firms surveyed by the World Bank. While workers in large firms are, on average, paid higher wages (figure 1.3), the relationship between firm size and the average wage rate disappears once other firm characteristics associated with size are accounted for, such as foreign ownership, exporting, or multiple-establishment status. Consistent with a recent study by Berlingieri, Calligaris, and Criscuolo (2018), firms with higher labor productivity pay higher wages. Exporters pay higher wages than nonexporters as well, which is consistent with the findings of other recent studies (Brambilla, Chauvin, and Porto 2015; Duda-Nyczak and Viegelahn 2018). A bundle of firm characteristics associated with size appears to have a stronger explanatory power over better jobs and higher wages than size per se.

Evidence from high-income countries further suggests that jobs in large firms are often better along a range of nonpecuniary dimensions. Longer queues for job posting and lower quit rates imply that jobs in large firms are more desirable (Katz and Summers 1989a, 1989b). Direct survey evidence suggests that employees of large firms have better work/life balance and satisfaction (Bloom, Kretschmer, and Van Reenen 2011). Evidence from several high-income countries shows that job stability increases with firm size (Garcia and van Soest 2016; Haltiwanger, Hyatt, and McEntarfer 2015). In turn, job stability influences future prospects, including the development of human capital and opportunities for advancement. Because large firms invest more in workers, they continue to pay higher wages to retain trained employees (Keith and McWilliams 1995; World Bank 2012). Learning on the job is one of the main benefits of industrial jobs over self-employment (De la Roca and Puga 2017). In countries where employment has been increasingly shifting toward outsourcing, the loss of opportunities for lifelong learning that go hand-in-hand with stable employment has started to affect career mobility and wage inequality (Dube and Kaplan 2010; Goldschmidt and Schmieder 2017; Irwin 2017; Katz and Krueger 2016). Given the prevalence of self-employment and informal wage employment in low- and middle-income countries—65 percent and 20 percent on average, respectively, according to recent estimates (Merotto, Weber, and Aterido 2018)—the quality of jobs provided becomes critical in assessing the contribution of large firms to development.

The International Income Distribution Data Set (I2D2) allows a closer look at jobs provided by large firms and yields additional insights into what is often argued to be the most important driver of poverty reduction (box 1.3). The evidence in I2D2 confirms that large firms in low- and middle-income countries provide higher-quality jobs in both pecuniary and nonpecuniary terms. On average, larger firms provide not only higher wages but also formal jobs, secure jobs, and benefits that smaller firms do not. In addition, the wage premium in large firms tends to be higher in lower-income countries. Finally, large firms appear to be more inclusive. That is, the large-firm wage premium tends to be higher for workers with less education.

FIGURE 1.8   Differences in the characteristics of large-firm jobs compared to small-firm jobs

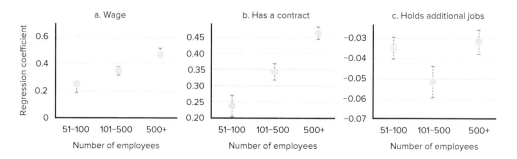

Source: Calculations based on World Bank International Income Distribution Data Set (I2D2) data (2018).
Note: The plots show coefficient estimates and 95% confidence interval from regressing job outcomes (wages, having a contract, holding additional jobs) on firm-size dummies. Large firms are defined as having 51–100, 101–500, or 500+ employees. Small firms are defined as having 0–50 employees.

How different are jobs in large firms?

The evidence presented in this report confirms some of the earlier findings on job quality in large firms. Beyond wages, large firms are significantly more likely to offer formal jobs; that is, a contract, health insurance, and social security benefits (figure 1.8). Workers in larger firms are also more likely to be employed full time and less likely to hold additional jobs. This is indirect evidence that large firms offer better job security, which is particularly important in light of the high rates of underemployment rather than unemployment in low- and middle-income countries (Merotto, Weber, and Aterido 2018).

FIGURE 1.9   Differences in the average education and skill mix between large and smaller firms

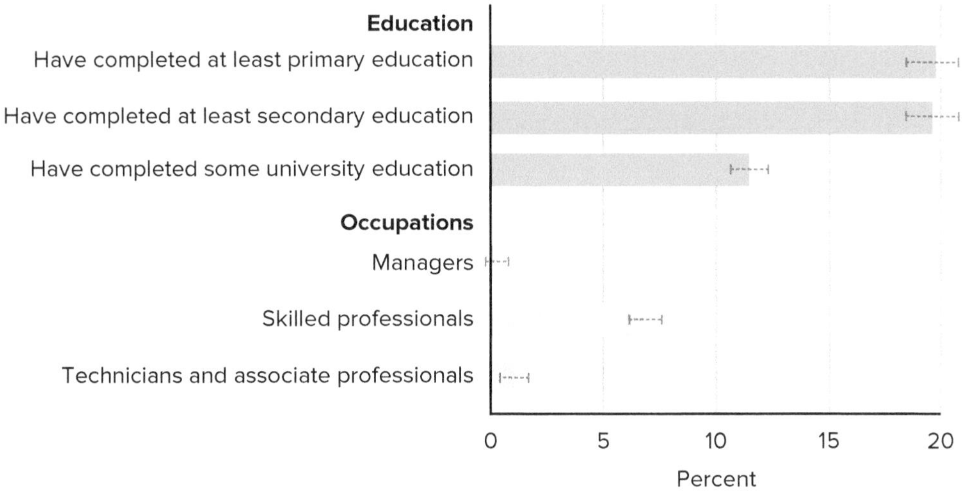

Source: Calculations based on World Bank International Income Distribution Data Set (I2D2) data (2018).
Note: The plots illustrate the marginal effect of being employed in large firms (100+ employees) on human capital. Results are derived from a regression of individual characteristics on firm-size dummies conditional on country, year, and industry fixed effects.

Worker selection drives part, but not all, of the observed premium. Indeed, workers in large firms are more educated and more likely to be employed in higher-skill occupations; on average, the share of skilled professionals is about 7 percentage points higher in large firms (figure 1.9). Nevertheless, the wage premium does not appear to be driven entirely by the selection of higher-ability workers into large firms. When controlling for worker characteristics such as age, gender, marital status, and education, the wage premium decreases but remains significant (appendix C, table C.1). Conditional on individual characteristics, the hourly wage is, on average, close to 22 percent higher in firms with more than 100 workers than in smaller competitors. Accounting for nonpecuniary benefits such as health and social security benefits, the large-firm wage premium remains close to 15 percent.

Large firms do not favor the least-educated workers, but they do offer better employment to workers with a basic education. Based on our evidence, there is no discernible wage premium for working in a large firm for workers with no education (figure 1.10). However, for workers with at least some education (a primary education), working in a large firm tends to imply a higher wage premium. On average, the wage gain from working in a large firm relative to an SME is 8–11 percentage points for workers with a complete primary education compared with workers with a secondary education and above.

FIGURE 1.10 Large-firm wage premium for different education levels

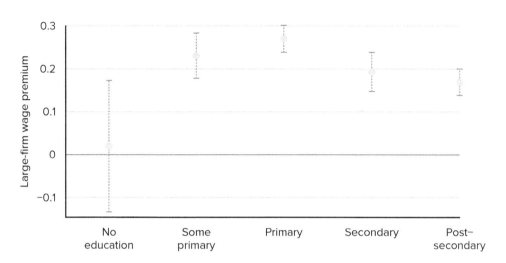

Source: Calculations based on World Bank International Income Distribution Data Set (I2D2) data (2018).
Note: The plot shows coefficient estimates and 95% confidence interval from regressing wages on firm size and education interactions, controlling for other individual characteristics and country and industry fixed effects.

These mixed results for different segments of the labor force could reflect the different contexts in which large firms operate. While manufacturing foreign direct investment, for example, has been found to have a significant positive effect on female educational attainment in Bangladesh, in Mexico the school dropout rate has been found to increase with local expansions of foreign multinationals (Atkin 2016; Heath and Mobarak 2015). These contrasting results are likely driven by differences in initial education levels and the skills content of manufacturing jobs in the two countries.

What drives the wage premium of large firms in low- and middle-income countries?

A sizable literature devoted to understanding the wage gap between large and small firms explores potential explanations that are consistent with perfect labor market clearing conditions or that rely on external regulatory constraints or market frictions (for a review, see Oi and Idson 1999; and Troske 1999). In the first line of reasoning, the premium might be driven by selection—that is, a higher wage is offered to attract higher-quality workers or to compensate for inferior working conditions in large firms. However, in studies where workers' ability could be taken into account, the evidence still points in the direction of a large-firm premium in wages, albeit a smaller one (Arai 2003; Brown and Medoff 1989; Criscuolo 2000; Söderbom, Teal, and Wambugu 2005). There is also a lack of evidence of worse working conditions in large firms. Controlling for proxies of working conditions does not eliminate the size premium (Schaffner 1998).

The second line of reasoning is related to more fundamental market imperfections related to so-called efficiency wages—referring to wages that overcompensate for labor output as an incentive to improve efficiency. The need for such an incentive might be that large firms face higher monitoring costs or find shirking more costly. Another explanation is that large firms might be more willing to pay higher wages to reduce turnover because of higher screening or training costs. Finally, large firms might find it optimal to share better returns arising from higher productivity or market power with workers (Oi and Idson 1999; Schaffner 1998; Söderbom, Teal, and Wambugu 2005; Velenchik 1997).

To the extent that it is driven by market frictions, a higher size-wage premium is costly and might explain why, in lower-income countries, it is harder for firms to grow large and therefore why a larger fraction of the labor force is employed in small establishments (Schaffner 1998). Our evidence confirms a previously documented stylized fact: across countries, the large-firm wage premium is generally higher at lower income levels, where market frictions are more intense. Figure 1.11 shows that the

FIGURE 1.11   Large-firm wage premiums, by country income level

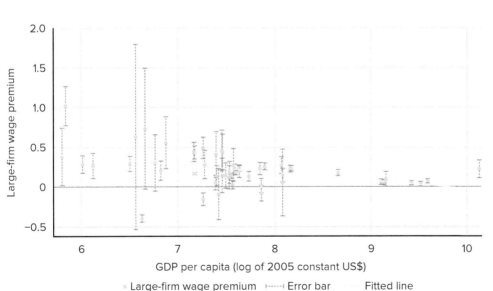

Source: Calculations based on World Bank International Income Distribution Data Set (I2D2) data (2018).
Note: The plots show coefficient estimates and 95% confidence interval from regressing wages on firm-size dummies at the country level, conditional on industry and year fixed effects.

magnitude of the premium is striking in several low-income countries, such as Niger in 2011 (more than 100 percent), the Comoros in 2013 (73 percent), and Tajikistan in 2009 (63 percent).

In theory, the size-cost differentials reflect fundamental differences between firms of different sizes—in their use of technologies or the way they are organized. For example, large firms might have a higher capital-to-labor ratio, more sophisticated technologies, a higher ratio of workers to owners, and a deeper organizational hierarchy than smaller firms, ultimately driving wider wage gaps (Oi and Idson 1999; Schaffner 1998; Söderbom, Teal, and Wambugu 2005). These differences would be more pronounced when there are more frictions in the labor or capital market and where information, risk, and contracting problems are more severe (Schaffner 1998; Söderbom, Teal, and Wambugu 2005).

There are several possible explanations at the macroeconomic level for why the wage premium is higher in lower-income countries. To the extent that wages are determined by labor productivity, the wage gap can reflect the productivity gap between small and large firms. This gap can be wider in lower-income countries if, for example, financial markets are incomplete. In such contexts, large firms might get better access to finance, which raises the productivity of workers. Consistent with this hypothesis, we find a negative relationship between a large-firm premium and countries' measure of private credit over gross domestic product (GDP).[6] Large firms can also pay more because they have more market power and are more profitable in markets with low contestability. We find some suggestive evidence of this hypothesis. The premium appears to fall with the degree of local competition, as reported in the World Economic Forum's Global Competitiveness Survey (Schwab and Sala-i-Martin 2017), which is consistent with the view that the premium is related to markups. This slope remains, even when controlling for GDP per capita. Another possible explanation pertains to segmented labor markets. If labor regulations are enforced less evenly in lower-income countries, then large firms might be more likely to comply and pay higher wages as a result. We find evidence supporting this hypothesis. The premium increases significantly with a measure of collective labor rights, even after controlling for GDP per capita. Nevertheless, the coefficient on GDP per capita remains negative and significant, suggesting that higher size premiums in lower-income countries are not driven entirely by labor market regulations (see appendix C for more details on these results).

These results suggest that higher market frictions in low- and middle-income countries might be a potential driver of the size/wage gap, which, in turn, might pose barriers to firm growth. High labor costs have been identified as one of the constraints on manufacturing growth in many Sub-Saharan African countries (Gelb, Meyer, and Ramachandran 2014). In Ethiopia, where there have been signs of the manufacturing sector taking off, working conditions in large

BOX 1.4 Job quality and development: Is there a trade-off?

According to Blattman and Dercon (2018), "For poor countries to develop, we simply do not know of any alternative to industrialization. The sooner that happens, the sooner the world will end extreme poverty. As we look at our results, we are conflicted: We do not want to see workers exposed to hazardous risks, but we also worry that regulating or improving the jobs too much too quickly will keep that industrial boom from happening. It is a difficult path to walk. But supporting insurance systems and encouraging companies to adopt modern management strategies and worker protections could be a way to travel that path faster and more safely."

industrial firms have often been found to be hazardous (Blattman and Dercon 2018). Is there a job quality/development trade-off for low-income countries on the path of industrialization? The answer might be a careful balancing of labor regulations and incentives to encourage companies to adopt modern management strategies that can both offer worker protection and improve labor productivity (box 1.4).

Macroeconomic outcomes are influenced by large-firm activity

Large firms look different, operate differently, and bring better development outcomes for both their owners and workers. But what do these premiums mean for aggregate development outcomes and progress in low- and middle-income countries?

A few "superstars" account for substantial shares of aggregate economic activity

While most of the evidence on the microeconomic foundations of aggregate outcomes comes from high-income countries due to data availability, the fact that few firms make up disproportionate shares of aggregate outcomes holds equally for low- and middle-income countries. Sutton (2002a), for example, was one of the first to document that a handful of leading industrial firms accounts for the bulk of export earnings in Ethiopia and Zambia. More systematic evidence on export "superstars" confirms that, globally, a small number of firms often accounts for most aggregate exports (Freund and Pierola 2015, 2016).

Disproportionate contributions of the largest formal firms to aggregate employment, output, and tax revenue are evident across 10 low- and middle-income countries in their industrial censuses (see figure 1.12 for the cumulative contribution of the top 20 firms in employment, value added, exports, and income tax to national aggregates). The numbers are striking; in

FIGURE 1.12   Cumulative contribution of the 20 largest firms in selected countries

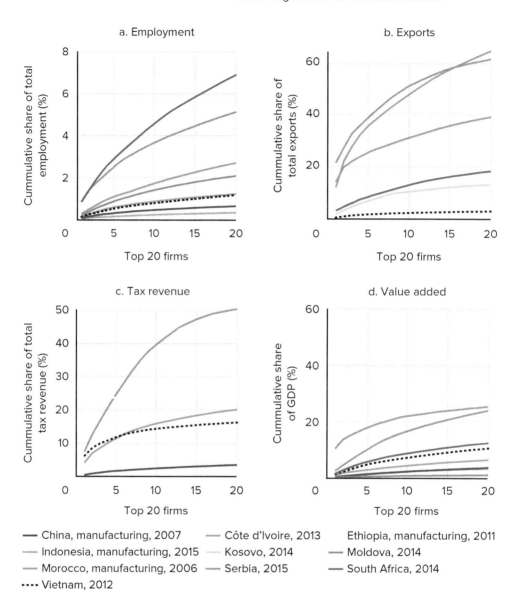

Sources: Calculations based on industrial census data from a selection of countries. Data on aggregate employment, gross domestic product (GDP), exports (goods and services), and tax on profits and capital gains are from the World Development Indicators.

Note: Aggregate employment data are missing for Kosovo. To check whether these results are driven by reporting errors, we conducted a similar exercise using data on the top 20 publicly listed firms and found similar results: sales of the few top firms account for a substantial share of countries' GDP.

Serbia, for example, the top 20 firms contribute more than 5 percent of national employment, 20 percent of GDP, 50 percent of all exports, and 50 percent of total revenue from profits and capital gains tax. In Ethiopia, the top manufacturing establishment contributes close to 10 percent of all GDP; more than half of total output in 2011 is accounted for by the top 20 firms. Even in large economies, individual firms make sizable contributions: the top 20 firms in Vietnam employ more than 1 percent of all workers, while the top 20 manufacturing firms in China and Indonesia produce between 3 and 4 percent of each country's total value added output.

What happens to these few largest firms can sway the whole economy. In some cases, a single firm expands enough to influence aggregate outcomes. Anecdotal evidence, such as the cases of Intel in Costa Rica and Nokia in Finland, suggests that the emergence of a single conglomerate can reshape the specialization and export intensity of a whole nation (Freund and Moran 2017). The close link between international trade flows and the success of individual firms is exemplified in the case of France: 20 percent of the variation in realized export intensity across sectors in the country is attributed to idiosyncratic shocks affecting the top firm in each sector. In turn, idiosyncratic firm dynamics account for a large share of the evolution of a country's comparative advantage over time (Gaubert and Itskhoki 2018).

Large firms contribute significantly to job creation and labor productivity growth

Contributions of large firms to macroeconomic outcomes are not only static: there is increasing evidence that large firms make up a disproportionate share of not only aggregate employment and productivity but also growth.[7]

Aggregate employment

Detailed data from industrial censuses as well as recent studies confirm that young and large firms are responsible for the bulk of net job creation in both high-income and low- and middle-income countries (Ayyagari, Demirgüç-Kunt, and Maksimovik 2014; Hallward-Driemeier and Rijkers 2013; Haltiwanger, Jarmin, and Miranda 2013; Van Biesebroeck 2005).

Evidence in this report corroborates the conclusion: despite their small numbers, large firms account for an important share of employment, both total and wage, as well as productivity growth. Large firms contribute more than 50 percent of net job creation across the sample of six countries for which we have both an industrial census and official statistics on employment growth (figure 1.13, panel a). Large firms can also contribute disproportionally

FIGURE 1.13   Cumulative contribution of large firms to aggregate employment

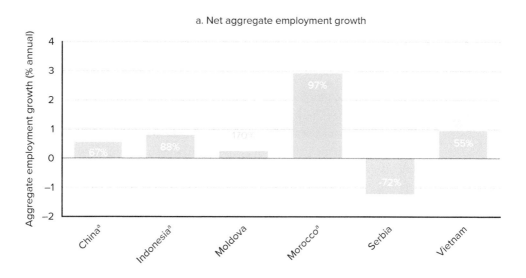

a. Net aggregate employment growth

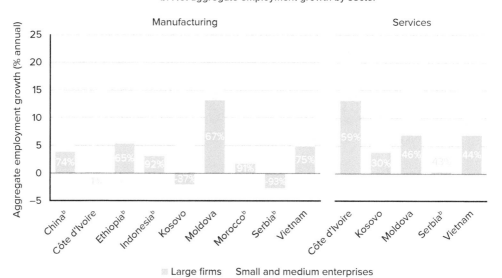

b. Net aggregate employment growth by sector

Large firms   Small and medium enterprises

Sources: Calculations based on industrial census data and World Development Indicators data from a selection of countries.
Note: The numbers that appear inside the bars indicate the jobs created by large firms as a share of total jobs created. For the representation of the aggregate economy in panel a, the total number of jobs created during the period studied in each country is from the World Bank World Development Indicators. The number of jobs created in large firms with (100+ employees) is from an industrial census. In panel b, both the aggregate number of jobs and the number of jobs created by large firms are from an industrial census. Annual growth is calculated over a different time period when data are available: China, 1999–2007; Côte d'Ivoire, 2004–13; Ethiopia, 2001 and 2011; Indonesia, 2010–15; Kosovo, 2007–14; Morocco, 1996–2006; Moldova, 2005–14; Serbia, 2007–15; and Vietnam, 2008–12.
a. Manufacturing only.
b. Censored census: in Ethiopia, 10+ employees, Indonesia, 20+ employees, Serbia 6+ employees, Morocco, 10+ employees, and China, revenue greater than ¥ 5 million.

34

to job losses and productivity slowdowns in bad times, as in the case of Serbia, although there is no general evidence about how macroeconomic shocks affect firms of different sizes.[8] On one hand, large firms might be more exposed to macroeconomic volatility and its transmission across borders through trade and foreign investment; on the other hand, larger firms are better placed to respond to shocks—by hoarding labor, for example—or by using cash reserves and inventories.

The variation is high across countries by sector of economic activity, with shares of large firms in employment growth being important in both sectors but generally higher in manufacturing than in services (figure 1.13, panel b). Estimates using exclusively the industrial censuses from the nine countries in our sample suffer from important imperfections: only part of the formal economy is surveyed, which corresponds in all countries to only a fraction of the actual jobs reported in official statistics. With the aggregate being substantially smaller, annual growth rates are significantly higher than the ones observed in official statistics (figure 1.13, panel a). In many cases, the census is censored by design, with only firms above a certain size or revenue threshold reported (see the note to figure 1.13). Finally, the time periods covered in each country vary substantially—before, during, or after the financial crisis, reflecting different shocks to the economy and consequently variable patterns that are hard to generalize. However imperfect, the distinct patterns across manufacturing and services remain rather intuitive, as scale in manufacturing sectors is associated more closely with productivity that allows firms to invest and grow employment.

The shares of large firms in wage employment—that is, excluding the self-employed from the aggregate number of workers—as well as over time, exhibit high variation because different sources were used for the estimation. More work is needed to assess the exact contribution of large firms across contexts, sectors of economic activity, time periods, and economies with high shares of informality.

Aggregate productivity

Because SMEs tend to contribute negatively to aggregate labor productivity, large firms often account for more than 100 percent of aggregate labor productivity growth throughout the sample period (figure 1.14, panel a). Nevertheless, our evidence suggests that, even when aggregate productivity growth is negative, the contribution of large firms often reduces aggregate productivity loss. There are a few exceptions, such as the case of Côte d'Ivoire in 2005–06 (figure 1.14, panel b).

FIGURE 1.14 Cumulative contribution of large firms to aggregate productivity

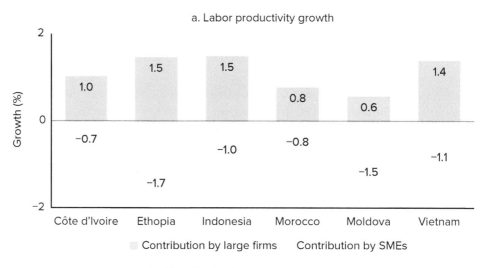
a. Labor productivity growth

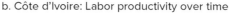

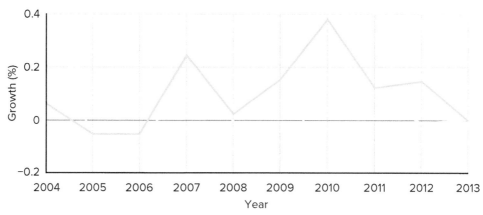
b. Côte d'Ivoire: Labor productivity over time

Aggregate labor productivity growth
Contribution of large firms to aggregate labor productivity growth

Source: Calculations based on industrial census data from a selection of countries (2018), following the methodology used by Van Biesebroeck 2005.
Note: SMEs = small and medium enterprises.

The sustainability of the macroeconomic contributions of large firms is a contribution in itself. Excluding periods of strong recessions, the literature suggests a fairly intuitive relationship between firm size and stability in employment, investment, and sales (Caves 1998; Sutton 1997, 2002b; Yeh 2017). The scale at which firms begin to be more resilient to fluctuations in the business cycle, however, remains an open question. In the United States, for example, lower cyclicality is only found among the largest firms—top 1 percent by size—which dominate the behavior of aggregate fluctuations because of their large share (Mehrotra and Crouzet 2017).

Smaller firms benefit from sizable spillovers to the wider economy

One important reason why large firms matter is their extensive linkages with other firms and customers. Evidence from France, for example, suggests that the largest firms are considerably different from the rest in the intensity of their direct linkages with foreign buyers and foreign affiliates. Because of their connectivity, large firms function as hubs for shocks to propagate throughout the production network, both domestically and internationally (Dosi et al. 2018; di Giovanni, Levchenko, and Mejean 2017; Magerman et al. 2016).

The evidence on various dimensions of the large-firm premiums highlights the channels through which large firms can have important spillover effects on the rest of the economy. Given that large firms are more likely to innovate and have higher productivity, they generate positive knowledge spillovers to other firms through agglomeration and supply chain linkages. Worker training and longer job tenure can lead to positive knowledge spillover through employee mobility.

Large firms' superior performance spills over to demand facing SMEs upstream in their value chains. In the Republic of Korea, for example, the sales of large firms have been shown to significantly affect the growth rate of vendor SMEs (Pyo and Lee 2018). A recent survey conducted in the United States shows that 7 out of 10 small businesses increased revenues and size within two years as a result of becoming part of a corporate supplier base. Evidence in Europe also suggests that SMEs' value added tends to benefit from positive shocks to the economic activity of larger firms. This positive spillover is attributed to strong structural links between large firms and SMEs in the region, such that the expansion of large firms translates into more business opportunities for SMEs. Beyond the direct effect of demand, there is also evidence that large enterprises can be important drivers of SME growth because interactions can lead to changes in small firms' organizational structure, management practices, efficiency, and access to finance (Ebeke and Eklou 2017; De Fuentes and Dutrénit 2013).

Although evidence from low- and middle-income countries is scarce to nonexistent, the experience of International Finance Corporation–supported linkages between lead firms and smaller firms suggests significantly positive effects. Beneficiaries of linkage initiatives on both sides often experience an increase in sales, productivity, export revenues, employment, and cost improvements, while indirect beneficiaries also experience positive spillovers through linkages to SMEs and other businesses servicing the value chain (World Bank 2018). Several countries, such as the Czech Republic and Malaysia, have also pursued active programs to support linkages of smaller firms with global value chains as suppliers to larger multinationals (World Bank 2019). However, evidence suggests that technical assistance to suppliers of large multinationals results in greater spillovers, highlighting the fact that most smaller firms in low-income countries require active support to take advantage of the opportunities offered by value chain linkages (Cusolito, Safadi, and Taglioni 2016).

In the long run, the growth of large, productive firms matters for aggregate growth

A central insight of the development literature is that long-term national income growth implies a transition from self-employment to wage employment and shifts in production from small toward larger, more productive firms (Gollin 2008; McMillan, Rodrik, and Sepulveda 2017; Schoar 2010). Empirically, there is substantial evidence that the average establishment size (and level of self-employment) changes dramatically as economies grow (Bento and Restuccia 2017; Gollin 2008). Income growth is often associated with the growth of firms: two-thirds of growth comes from the expansion of existing organizations rather than the creation of new ones (Rajan and Zingales 1998).

Firm size and productivity translate into aggregate growth through efficient resource allocation. Countries are richer when they can produce goods and services more productively. Aggregate productivity growth, in turn, depends on the extent to which resources shift toward productive firms. The ability of high-productivity firms to grow, which results in large *productive* firms, explains a great deal of the differences in country productivity and tends to increase with level of income in both high-income and low- and middle-income countries (Bento and Restuccia 2017; Freund 2016; Hsieh and Klenow 2009, 2014). To answer these questions, and specifically the cross-country differences in the numbers of large productive firms and the ways they grow, we turn to the chapters that follow.

Notes

1 | The World Bank Enterprise Surveys are establishment-level surveys based on face-to-face interviews with owners or top managers. The surveys are designed to provide a representative sample of firms in the nonagricultural, nonextractive formal private economy with five or more employees and to ensure that the data are comparable across countries and time. For more details on the methodology, see http://www.enterprisesurveys.org/methodology. The Enterprise Survey data from high-income economies (as classified by the World Bank for the year in which the survey was conducted) are excluded from the analysis.

2 | The relationship is stronger when productivity is measured in value added rather than sales per employee. Notably, when defining large firms at larger thresholds of employment, the overlap deteriorates, possibly due to decreasing marginal returns to constrained capital or simply the lack of contestability at the very right side of the firm-size distribution. A more inclusive definition of "large," such as the definition of large firms as having 100+ employees that is used in this report, captures this relationship well.

3 | The figures presented in this chapter represent coefficients on the dummy variable for large firms, taking into account only the firms' country and sector of operation. We use distinct shading in the charts whenever the results change substantively after controlling for the full set of firm characteristics and also note such changes in the text. The analysis based on the World Bank Enterprise Surveys is not meant to suggest a causal relationship between outcomes and firm size. Although we do control for a series of firm characteristics, along with country and sector fixed effects, the regressions do not identify causal effects.

4 | Figure 1.3 suggests lower levels of capital intensity (ratio of capital use to output) among large firms. However, once we account for firm characteristics and the use of other inputs in production (specifically, material and labor inputs), large firms are found to use capital more intensively than SMEs.

5 | This relationship between firm size and age holds even after controlling for other firm characteristics and aspects of the environment in which they operate. The firm characteristics we control for are foreign ownership, multiple-establishment status, exporting status, the top manager's experience in the sector, legal form, and the firm's size when it began operating.

6 | The evidence is weak, however. Regressing large-firm premiums on both GDP per capita and private credit per GDP at the country level yields insignificant results and a very small estimated coefficient on credit per GDP. This result could be due to the relatively small sample of countries.

7 | The positive correlation between employment and productivity growth during business cycles was an established theoretical and empirical fact until recently (Gali 1999; García-Cabo Herrero 2013; Mortensen and Pissarides 1994). The cases of Europe and the United States, where productivity growth over the last two decades has been associated with rising unemployment, have cast doubts on the validity of the assertion, although explanations have thus far revolved around idiosyncratic developments in the two economies rather than structural relationships between employment and productivity.

8 | Evidence confirms the same patterns in the United States: employment in large firms was affected more adversely than employment in small firms during recent recessions (Kudlyak, Price, and Sánchez 2010; Moscarini and Postel-Vinay 2009).

References

Alvarez, Roberto, and Ricardo A. Lopez. 2005. "Exporting and Performance: Evidence from Chilean Plants." *Canadian Journal of Economics/Revue Canadienne d'Économique* 38 (4): 1384–400.

Andersen, Otto. 1993. "On the Internationalization Process of Firms: A Critical Analysis." *Journal of International Business Studies* 24 (2): 209–31.

Antoniades, Alexis. 2015. "Heterogeneous Firms, Quality, and Trade." *Journal of International Economics* 95 (2): 263–73.

Anyadike-Danes, Michael, Carl-Magnus Bjuggren, Sandra Gottschalk, Werner Hölzl, Dan Johansson, Mike Maliranta, and Anja Myrann. 2015. "An International Cohort Comparison of Size Effects on Job Growth." *Small Business Economics* 44 (4): 821–44.

Arai, Mahmood. 2003. "Wages, Profits, and Capital Intensity: Evidence from Matched Worker-Firm Data." *Journal of Labor Economics* 21 (3): 593–618.

Atkin, David. 2016. "Endogenous Skill Acquisition and Export Manufacturing in Mexico." *American Economic Review* 106 (8): 2046–85.

Autio, Erkko, Harry J. Sapienza, and James G. Almeida. 2000. "Effects of Age at Entry, Knowledge Intensity, and Imitability on International Growth." *Academy of Management Journal* 43 (5): 909–24.

Ayyagari, Meghana, Aslı Demirgüç-Kunt, and Vojislav Maksimovic. 2011. "Small vs. Young Firms across the World: Contribution to Employment, Job Creation, and Growth." Policy Research Working Paper 5631, World Bank, Washington, DC.

Ayyagari, Meghana, Aslı Demirgüç-Kunt, and Vojislav Maksimovic. 2014. "Who Creates Jobs in Developing Countries?" *Small Business Economics* 43 (1): 75–99.

Barth, Erling, James Davis, and Richard B. Freeman. 2018. "Augmenting the Human Capital Earnings Equation with Measures of Where People Work." *Journal of Labor Economics* 36 (S1): S71–S97.

Bayard, Kimberly, and Kenneth R. Troske. 1999. "Examining the Employer-Size Wage Premium in the Manufacturing, Retail Trade, and Service Industries Using Employer-Employee Matched Data." *American Economic Review* 89 (2): 99–103.

Bento, Pedro, and Diego Restuccia. 2017. "Misallocation, Establishment Size, and Productivity." *American Economic Journal: Macroeconomics* 9 (3): 267–303.

Berlingieri, Giuseppe, Patrick Blanchenay, and Chiara Criscuolo. 2017. "The Great Divergence(s)." OECD Science, Technology, and Industry Policy Paper 39, OECD Publishing, Paris.

Berlingieri, Giuseppe, Sara Calligaris, and Chiara Criscuolo. 2018. "The Productivity-Wage Premium: Does Size Still Matter in a Service Economy?" *AEA Papers and Proceedings* 108 (May): 328–33.

Bernard, Andrew B., J. Bradford Jensen, Stephen J. Redding, and Peter K. Schott. 2007. "Firms in International Trade." *Journal of Economic Perspectives* 21 (3): 105–30.

Blattman, Christopher, and Stefan Dercon. 2018. "The Impacts of Industrial and Entrepreneurial Work on Income and Health: Experimental Evidence from Ethiopia." *American Economic Journal: Applied Economics* 10 (3): 1–38.

Bloom, Nicholas, Benn Eifert, Aprajit Mahajan, David McKenzie, and John Roberts. 2013. "Does Management Matter? Evidence from India." *Quarterly Journal of Economics* 128 (1): 1–51.

Bloom, Nicholas, Christos Genakos, Raffaella Sadun, and John Van Reenen. 2012. "Management Practices across Firms and Countries." NBER Working Paper 17850, National Bureau of Economic Research, Cambridge, MA.

Bloom, Nicolas, Tobias Kretschmer, and John Van Reenen. 2011. "Are Family-Friendly Workplace Practices a Valuable Firm Resource?" *Strategic Management Journal* 32 (4): 343–67.

Bloom, Nicholas, and John Van Reenen. 2007. "Measuring and Explaining Management Practices across Firms and Countries." *Quarterly Journal of Economics* 122 (4): 1351–408.

Bloom, Nicholas, and John Van Reenen. 2010. "Why Do Management Practices Differ across Firms and Countries?" *Journal of Economic Perspectives* 24 (1): 203–24.

Bottini, Novella, and Margit Molnar. 2010. "How Large Are Competitive Pressures in Services Markets? Estimation of Mark-ups for Selected OECD Countries." *OECD Journal: Economic Studies* 1: 1–51.

Bouis, Romain, and Caroline C. Klein. 2008. "La concurrence favorise-t-elle les gains de productivité ? Une analyse sectorielle dans les pays d l'OCDE." *Economie et statistique* 419 (1): 73–99. Institut National de la Statistique et des Études Économiques (INSEE), Paris.

Boycko, Maxim, Andrei Shleifer, and Robert W. Vishny. 1996. "A Theory of Privatization." *Economic Journal* 106 (435): 309–19.

Brambilla, Irene, Nicolas Depetris Chauvin, and Guido Porto. 2015. "Wage and Employment Gains from Exports: Evidence from Developing Countries." CEPII Working Paper 2015-28, Centre d'Études Prospectives et d'Informations Internationales, Paris.

Brown, Charles, and James Medoff. 1989. "The Employer Size-Wage Effect." *Journal of Political Economy* 97 (5): 1027–59.

Carpenter, Mason A., and James W. Fredrickson. 2001. "Top Management Teams, Global Strategic Posture, and the Moderating Role of Uncertainty." *Academy of Management Journal* 44 (3): 533–45.

Caves, Richard E. 1998. "Industrial Organization and New Findings on the Turnover and Mobility of Firms." *Journal of Economic Literature* 36 (4): 1947–82.

Christopoulou, Rebekka, and Philip Vermeulen. 2008. "Mark-ups in the Euro Area and the US over the Period: 1981–2004: A Comparison of 50 Sectors." European Central Bank Working Paper 856, European Central Bank, Frankfurt.

Criscuolo, Chiara. 2000. "Employer Size-Wage Effect: A Critical Review and an Econometric Analysis." Working Paper 277, Dipartimento di Economia Politica, Universita degli Studi di Siena, Siena.

Criscuolo, Chiara, Peter N. Gal, and Carlo Menon. 2014. "The Dynamics of Employment Growth: New Evidence from 18 Countries." OECD Science, Technology, and Industry Policy Paper 14, OECD Publishing, Paris.

Cusolito, Ana Paula, Raed Safadi, and Daria Taglioni. 2016. *Inclusive Global Value Chains: Policy Options for Small and Medium Enterprises and Low-Income Countries.* Directions in Development. Washington, DC: World Bank

De Fuentes, Claudia, and Gabriela Dutrénit. 2013. "SMEs' Absorptive Capacities and Large Firms' Knowledge Spillovers: Micro Evidence from the Machining Industry in Mexico." *Institutions and Economies* (formerly *International Journal of Institutions and Economies*) 5 (1): 1–30.

De la Roca, Jorge, and Diego Puga. 2017. "Learning by Working in Big Cities." *Review of Economic Studies* 84 (1): 106–42.

Demsetz, Harold, and Kenneth Lehn. 1985. "The Structure of Corporate Ownership: Causes and Consequences." *Journal of Political Economy* 93 (6): 1155–77.

DeWenter, Kathryn L., and Paul H. Malatesta. 2001. "State-Owned and Privately Owned Firms: An Empirical Analysis of Profitability, Leverage, and Labor Intensity." *American Economic Review* 91 (1): 320–34.

di Giovanni, Julian, Andrei A. Levchenko, and Isabelle Mejean. 2017. "Large Firms and International Business Cycle Comovement." *American Economic Review* 107 (5): 598–602.

Dominguez, Luis V., and Carlos G. Sequeira. 1993. "Determinants of LDC Exporters' Performance: A Cross-National Study." *Journal of International Business Studies* 24 (1): 19–40.

Dosi, Giovanni, Mauro Napoletano, Andrea Roventini, and Tania Treibich. 2018. "Debunking the Granular Origins of Aggregate Fluctuations: From Real Business Cycles Back to Keynes." *Journal of Evolutionary Economics* 29 (1): 67–90.

Dube, Arindrajit, and Ethan Kaplan. 2010. "Does Outsourcing Reduce Wages in the Low-Wage Service Occupations? Evidence from Janitors and Guards." *ILR Review* 63 (2): 287–306.

Duda-Nyczak, Marta, and Christian Viegelahn. 2018. "Exporting, Importing, and Wages in Africa: Evidence from Matched Employer–Employee Data." ILO Working Paper 26, International Labour Organization, Geneva.

Ebeke, Christian, and Kodjovi Eklou. 2017. "The Granular Origins of Macroeconomic Fluctuations in Europe." IMF Working Paper 17/229, International Monetary Fund, Washington, DC, November.

EBRD (European Bank for Reconstruction and Development). 2018. "Sustaining Growth, Transition Report 2017–18." EBRD, London.

Eurostat and OECD (Organisation for Economic Co-operation and Development). 2007. *Eurostat-OECD Manual on Business Demography Statistics.* Paris: OECD.

Fafchamps, Marcel, and Måns Söderbom. 2006. "Wages and Labor Management in African Manufacturing." *Journal of Human Resources* 41 (2): 356–79.

Freund, Caroline. 2016. *Rich People Poor Countries: The Rise of Emerging-Market Tycoons and Their Mega Firms.* Washington, DC: Peterson Institute for International Economics.

Freund, Caroline, and Theodore H. Moran. 2017. "Multinational Investors as Export Superstars: How Emerging-Market Governments Can Reshape Comparative Advantage." Working Paper 17-1, Peterson Institute for International Economics, Washington, DC.

Freund, Caroline, and Martha Denisse Pierola. 2015. "Export Superstars." *Review of Economics and Statistics* 97 (5): 1023–32.

Freund, Caroline, and Martha Denisse Pierola. 2016. "The Origins and Dynamics of Export Superstars." Working Paper 16-11, Peterson Institute for International Economics, Washington, DC.

Gali, Jordi. 1999. "Technology, Employment, and the Business Cycle: Do Technology Shocks Explain Aggregate Fluctuations?" *American Economic Review* 89 (1): 249–71.

Garcia, Nagore A., and Arthur van Soest. 2016. "New Job Matches and Their Stability before and during the Crisis." Discussion Paper 2016-033, Tilburg University, Center for Economic Research, Tilburg.

García-Cabo Herrero, Joaquín. 2013. "Unemployment and Productivity over the Business Cycle: Evidence from OECD Countries." Master's thesis CEMFI 1301, Center for Monetary and Financial Studies, Frankfurt.

Gaubert, Cecile, and Oleg Itskhoki. 2018. "Granular Comparative Advantage." NBER Working Paper 24807, National Bureau of Economic Research, Cambridge, MA.

Gelb, Alan, Christian J. Meyer, and Vijaya Ramachandran. 2014. "Development as Diffusion: Manufacturing Productivity and Sub-Saharan Africa's Missing Middle." CGD Working Paper 357, Center for Global Development, Washington, DC.

Goldschmidt, Deborah, and Johannes F. Schmieder. 2017. "The Rise of Domestic Outsourcing and the Evolution of the German Wage Structure." *Quarterly Journal of Economics* 132 (3): 1165–217.

Gollin, Douglas. 2008. "Nobody's Business but My Own: Self-Employment and Small Enterprise in Economic Development." *Journal of Monetary Economics* 55 (2): 219–33.

Goswami, Arti Grover, Denis Medvedev, and Ellen Olafsen. 2019. *High-Growth Firms: Facts, Fiction, and Policy Options for Emerging Economies*. Washington, DC: World Bank.

Grossman, Sanford J., and Oliver D. Hart. 1986. "The Costs and Benefits of Ownership: A Theory of Vertical and Lateral Integration." *Journal of Political Economy* 94 (4): 691–719.

Hallward-Driemeier, Mary, and Bob Rijkers. 2013. "Do Crises Catalyze Creative Destruction? Firm-Level Evidence from Indonesia." *Review of Economics and Statistics* 95 (5): 1788–810.

Haltiwanger, John, Henry Hyatt, and Erika McEntarfer. 2015. "Cyclical Reallocation of Workers across Employers by Firm Size and Firm Wage." NBER Working Paper 21235, National Bureau of Economic Research, Cambridge, MA.

Haltiwanger, John, Ron S. Jarmin, and Javier Miranda. 2013. "Who Creates Jobs? Small versus Large versus Young." *Review of Economics and Statistics* 95 (2): 347–61.

Headd, Brian, and Bruce Kirchhoff. 2009. "The Growth, Decline, and Survival of Small Businesses: An Exploratory Study of Life Cycles." *Journal of Small Business Management* 47 (4): 531–50.

Heath, Rachel, and A Mushafiq Mobarak. 2015. "Manufacturing Growth and the Lives of Bangladeshi Women." *Journal of Development Economics* 115 (July): 1–15.

Høj, Jens, Miguel Jimenez, Maria Maher, Giuseppe Nicoletti, and Michael Wise. 2007. "Product Market Competition in the OECD Countries: Taking Stock and Moving Forward." OECD Economics Department Working Paper 575, OECD, Paris.

Hsieh, Chang-Tai, and Peter J. Klenow. 2009. "Misallocation and Manufacturing TFP in China and India." *Quarterly Journal of Economics* 124 (4): 1403–48.

Hsieh, Chang-Tai, and Peter J. Klenow. 2014. "The Life Cycle of Plants in India and Mexico." *Quarterly Journal of Economics* 129 (3): 1035–84.

Irwin, Neil. 2017. "To Understand Rising Inequality, Consider the Janitor at Two Top Companies, Then and Now." *New York Times*. September 3. https://www.nytimes.com/2017/09/03/upshot/to-understand-rising-inequality-consider-the-janitors-at-two-top-companies-then-and-now.html.

Javorcik, Beate Smarzynska. 2004. "Does Foreign Direct Investment Increase the Productivity of Domestic Firms? In Search of Spillovers through Backward Linkages." *American Economic Review* 94 (3): 605–27.

Katz, Lawrence F., and Alan B. Krueger. 2016. "The Rise and Nature of Alternative Work Arrangements in the United States, 1995–2015." NBER Working Paper 22667, National Bureau of Economic Research, Cambridge, MA.

Katz, Lawrence F., and Lawrence H. Summers. 1989a. "Can Interindustry Wage Differentials Justify Strategic Trade Policy?" In *Trade Policies for International Competitiveness,* edited by Robert C. Feenstra, chap. 3. Cambridge, MA: National Bureau of Economic Research.

Katz, Lawrence F., and Lawrence H. Summers. 1989b. "Industry Rents: Evidence and Implications." *Brookings Papers on Economic Activity* 20: 209–75.

Keith, Kristen, and Abagail McWilliams. 1995. "The Wage Effects of Cumulative Job Mobility." *ILR Review* 49 (1): 121–37.

Kudlyak, Marianna, David A. Price, and Juan M. Sánchez. 2010. "The Responses of Small and Large Firms to Tight Credit Shocks: The Case of 2008 through the Lens of Gertler and Gilchrist (1994)." *Federal Reserve Bank of Richmond: Economic Brief* 10 (10): 1–3.

Leung, Danny, Césaire Meh, and Yaz Terajima. 2008. "Firm Size and Productivity." Staff Working Paper 08-45, Bank of Canada, Ottawa.

Liu, Qigui, Gary Sang Tian, and Xiaoming Wang. 2011. "The Effect of Ownership Structure on Leverage Decision: New Evidence from Chinese Listed Firms." *Journal of the Asia Pacific Economy* 16 (2): 254–76.

Lucas, Robert E., Jr. 1978. "On the Size Distribution of Business Firms." *Bell Journal of Economics* 9 (2): 508–23.

Magerman, Glenn, Karoline De Bruyne, Emmanuel Dhyne, and Jan Van Hove. 2016. "Heterogeneous Firms and the Micro Origins of Aggregate Fluctuations." ECARES 2016-35, Université Libre de Bruxelles, Brussels.

Mazumdar, Dipak, and Ata Mazaheri. 2002. *Wages and Employment in Africa*. Burlington, VT: Ashgate.

McDougall, Patricia P., and Benjamin M. Oviatt. 2000. "International Entrepreneurship: The Intersection of Two Research Paths." *Academy of Management Journal* 43 (5): 902–06.

McMillan, Margaret, Dani Rodrik, and Claudia Sepulveda. 2017. "Structural Change, Fundamentals, and Growth: A Framework and Case Studies." NBER Working Paper 23378, National Bureau of Economic Research, Cambridge, MA.

Mehrotra, Neil, and Nicolas Crouzet. 2017. "Small and Large Firms over the Business Cycle." Paper prepared for the 2017 meeting of the Society for Economic Dynamics, Edinburgh, June 22–24.

Merotto, Dino, Michael Weber, and Reyes Aterido. 2018. "Pathways to Better Jobs in IDA Countries: Findings from Jobs Diagnostics." Job Series 14, World Bank, Washington, DC.

Moore, Henry L. 1911. *Laws of Wages: An Essay in Statistical Economics*. New York: Macmillan.

Mortensen, Dale T., and Christopher A. Pissarides. 1994. "Job Creation and Job Destruction in the Theory of Unemployment." *Review of Economic Studies* 61 (3): 397–415.

Moscarini, Giuseppe, and Fabien Postel-Vinay. 2009. "The Timing of Labor Market Expansions: New Facts and a New Hypothesis." In *NBER Macroeconomics Annual 2008,* vol. 23, edited by Daron Acemoglu, Kenneth Rogoff, and Michael Woodford, 1–52. Chicago: University of Chicago Press.

OECD (Organisation for Economic Co-operation and Development). Various years. DynEmp (Measuring Job Creation by Start-ups and Young Firms) database. Paris: OECD, Directorate for Science, Technology, and Innovation. http://www.oecd.org/sti/dynemp.htm.

OECD (Organisation for Economic Co-operation and Development). Various years. Orbis database. Paris: OECD.

Oi, Walter Y., and Todd L. Idson. 1999. "Firm Size and Wages." In *Handbook of Labor Economics*, vol. 3B, edited by Orley Ashenfelter and David Card, 2165–214. Amsterdam: Elsevier Science.

Olney, William W. 2016. "Impact of Corruption on Firm-Level Export Decisions." *Economic Inquiry* 54 (2): 1105–27.

Park, Younsuk, Jaeun Shin, and Taejong Kim. 2010. "Firm Size, Age, Industrial Networking, and Growth: A Case of the Korean Manufacturing Industry." *Small Business Economics* 35 (2): 153–68.

Poschke, Markus. 2018. "The Firm Size Distribution across Countries and Skill-Biased Change in Entrepreneurial Technology." *American Economic Journal: Macroeconomics* 10 (3): 1–41.

Pyo, Hanhyung, and Sangheon Lee. 2018. "Are There Spillover Effects of Large Firms' Growth in the Supply Chain Networks? Evidence from the Korean Economy." *Applied Economic Letters* 25 (17): 1208–11.

Rajan, Raghuram G., and Luigi Zingales. 1998. "Power in a Theory of the Firm." *Quarterly Journal of Economics* 113 (2): 387–432.

Regis, Paulo J. 2018. "The Extensive and Intensive Margins of Exports of Firms in Developing and Emerging Countries." *International Review of Economics and Finance* 56 (July): 39–49.

Sapienza, Harry J., Erkko Autio, Gerard George, and Shaker A. Zahra. 2006. "A Capabilities Perspective on the Effects of Early Internationalization on Firm Survival and Growth." *Academy of Management Review* 31 (4): 914–33.

Schaffner, Julie. 1998. "Premiums to Employment in Larger Establishments: Evidence from Peru." *Journal of Development Economics* 55 (1): 81–113.

Schoar, Antoinette. 2010. "The Divide between Subsistence and Transformational Entrepreneurship." In *Innovation Policy and the Economy,* vol. 10, edited by Josh Lerner and Scott Stern, 57–81. Chicago: University of Chicago Press.

Schwab, Klaus, and Xavier Sala-i-Martin. 2017. *Global Competitiveness Report 2017–2018*. Geneva: World Economic Forum.

Söderbom, Måns, Francis Teal, and Anthony Wambugu. 2005. "Unobserved Heterogeneity and the Relation between Earnings and Firm Size: Evidence from Two Developing Countries." *Economic Letters* 87 (2): 153–59.

Sutton, John. 1997. "Gibrat's Legacy." *Journal of Economic Literature* 35 (1): 40–59.

Sutton, John. 2002a. "Rich Trades, Scarce Capabilities: Industrial Development Revisited." *Economic and Social Review, Economic and Social Studies* 33 (1): 1–22.

Sutton, John. 2002b. "The Variance of Firm Growth Rates: The 'Scaling' Puzzle." *Physica A* 312 (3): 577–90.

Ter Wengel, Jan, and Edgar Rodriguez. 2006. "SME Export Performance in Indonesia after the Crisis." *Small Business Economics* 26 (1): 25–37.

Troske, Kenneth R. 1999. "Evidence on the Employer Size-Wage Premium from Worker-Establishment Matched Data." *Review of Economics and Statistics* 81 (1): 15–26.

Van Biesebroeck, Johannes. 2005. "Firm Size Matters: Growth and Productivity Growth in African Manufacturing." *Economic Development and Cultural Change* 53 (3): 548–83.

Velenchik, Ann D. 1997. "Government Intervention, Efficiency Wages, and the Employer Size Wage Effect in Zimbabwe." *Journal of Development Economics* 53 (2): 305–38.

World Bank. 2012. *World Development Report 2013: Jobs.* Washington, DC: World Bank.

World Bank. 2018. *Partnership for Growth: Linking Large Firms and Agro-Processing SMEs.* Washington, DC: World Bank.

World Bank. 2019. *World Development Report 2019: The Changing Nature of Work.* Washington, DC: World Bank.

World Bank. Various years. International Income Distribution Data Set (I2D2). Washington, DC: World Bank.

World Bank. Various years. World Bank Enterprise Surveys database. Washington, DC: World Bank.

World Bank. Various years. World Development Indicators database. Washington, DC: World Bank.

Yang, Chih-Hai, Jong-Rong Chen, and Wen-Bin Chuang. 2004. "Technology and Export Decision." *Small Business Economics* 22 (5): 349–64.

Yang, Chih-Hai, and Ku-Hsieh Chen. 2009. "Are Small Firms Less Efficient?" *Small Business Economics* 32 (4): 375–95.

Yasuda, Takehiko. 2005. "Firm Growth, Size, Age, and Behavior in Japanese Manufacturing." *Small Business Economics* 24 (1): 1–15.

Yeh, Chen. 2017. "Are Firm-Level Idiosyncratic Shocks Important for U.S. Aggregate Volatility?" CES-Working Paper 17-23, Center for Economic Studies, United States Census Bureau, Washington, DC.

Zahra, Shaker A., R. Duane Ireland, and Michael A. Hitt. 2000. "International Expansion by New Venture Firms: International Diversity, Mode of Market Entry, Technological Learning, and Performance." *Academy of Management Journal* 43 (5): 925–50.

2. The "missing top"

The question of whether low- and middle-income countries have enough large firms has no straightforward answer. In this chapter, we investigate the number of large firms in a cross-country comparative manner. Are their numbers comparable to figures observed elsewhere in the world? Taking market size, sectoral mix, and overall firm population as given, do the number and size of large firms deviate systematically from our expectations and, if so, in which direction?

While lower-income markets tend to host smaller firms on average, pairwise comparisons of countries at different levels of development suggests that a gap might exist in relative terms as well. In 2016, for example, for every 100 medium-sized firms—defined as firms with 20–99 employees—there were more than 20 large firms operating in the nonagricultural sector in the United States, as opposed to less than 9 in Indonesia, a lower-middle-income country with roughly the same population.[1] A closer study of segments of the firm-size distribution in country pairs suggests that what is missing in low- and middle-income countries is the larger among large firms as well as the more productive and outward-oriented firms. If an "optimal" number of large firms is defined proportionately against the number of smaller firms, then low- and middle-income countries have fewer large firms than is common in the rest of the world. Our findings highlight a "missing top" rather than a "missing middle"—a gap to the right of the firm-size distribution in low- and middle-income countries.

Lower-income countries tend to have smaller firms

The empirical association between firm scale and level of development is an old observation. The prevalence of small-scale production correlates negatively with per capita income levels not only across countries but also within countries throughout time (Banarji 1978; Liedholm and Mead 1987; Little 1987; Steel 1993; Tybout 2000). Yet establishments are not proportionally smaller in lower-income countries: the gap is believed to exist in the middle of the firm-size distribution. A so-called "dual-economy" view of low- and middle-income countries hosting very many small firms and a few large firms operating differently under different constraints, which was described as early as the 1950s (Lewis 1954), gave rise to the so-called "missing middle" hypothesis, followed by an array of possible explanations.

Recent empirical investigations of the relationship between economic development and establishment size have benefited from better data, yet have reached no uniform conclusions. A recent study, for example, finds a positive relationship between establishment size and development (Poschke 2018), while earlier work highlights opposite patterns (Alfaro, Charlton, and Kanczuk 2008; Bollard, Klenow, and Li 2014). How comparable these estimates are remains an open question. Indeed, estimates might be biased by measurement error or the use of different methodologies to aggregate data at the higher levels typically reported in official statistics.

The most comprehensive recent account based on comparable country-level economic censuses and surveys from 134 countries suggests that firms are, on average, smaller in lower-income markets than in richer ones (Bento and Restuccia 2020). Using the average number of persons engaged per establishment, a 5 percent higher gross domestic product (GDP) per capita is associated with a more than 1 percent higher average establishment size. The positive, significant correlation between establishment size and income becomes even stronger when small countries with populations less than 500,000 are omitted from the estimation sample.

High-income countries drive a disproportionate amount of variation in this relationship. Dividing countries into two groups, depending on whether they are considered high income or not, helps to illustrate this point.[2] The estimated correlation between GDP per capita and establishment size for the group of low- and middle-income countries is 0.39, which is significant at the 1 percent level (figure 2.1), while the estimated correlation is higher for high-income countries, where a 1 percent increase in GDP per capita is associated with a 0.50 percent higher average establishment size. An equivalent increase in GDP per capita is then associated with larger establishment size in high-income countries.

FIGURE 2.1 Average size of nonagricultural establishments and GDP per capita, by country income level

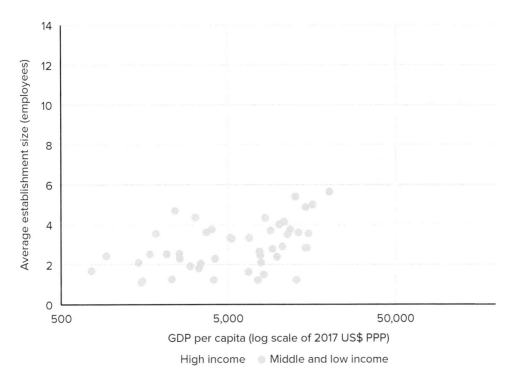

Source: Illustration based on Bento and Restuccia 2020.
Note: Manufacturing data were collected for as many years as possible for each country from 2000 to 2012, while service data were collected for the year closest to 2007. Countries were identified as high-income following the World Bank Income Classification 2017. PPP = purchasing power parity.

While fairly intuitive, the association remains coarse. GDP per capita captures a great variety of market characteristics that might be reflected in establishment size. Patterns drawn from business censuses bring a wealth of additional insights.

The gap is in the larger among large firms

Information about the universe of firms in low- and middle-income countries is scarce. Suggestive evidence on firm-size distributions often relies on pair-wise comparisons between countries that carry out business censuses and are of similar size, yet are at different levels of development (Alfaro and Chari 2014; Hsieh and Olken 2014).

FIGURE 2.2 Distribution of average firm-level employment in selected middle- and lower-income countries

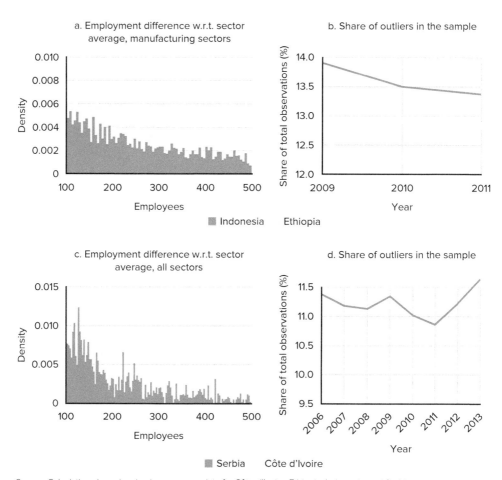

Source: Calculations based on business census data for Côte d'Ivoire, Ethiopia, Indonesia, and Serbia.
Note: The industrial censuses for Ethiopia and Indonesia only cover the manufacturing sector. w.r.t. = with regard to.

To shed light on whether richer economies have a different population of larger firms, we follow this approach and compare the distribution of firm-level employment for two pairs of similar-size countries at different stages of development: Côte d'Ivoire and Serbia, on one hand, and Ethiopia and Indonesia, on the other. The size of markets as well as the mix of activities tracked in the surveys provide a starting point for assessing the number of large firms operating in the market.

Expressing all observations relative to the sectoral and market average consistently shows that lower-income markets have fewer larger among large firms. In Serbia, for example, an upper-middle-income country with a population of 7 million, the frequency of firms that are larger than the average in each given sector, is higher relative to Côte d'Ivoire, a lower-middle-income country with a population of 24 million (see figure 2.2, panels b and d, for the distribution of average firm-level employment with respect to sector and year average for the two countries). Evidence for manufacturing in Ethiopia and Indonesia between 2009 and 2011 exhibits a similar pattern. In this pair, it is more likely to find firms that are larger than the sector average in Indonesia, the richer economy. The frequency distribution of differences in employment with respect to the sector average for Indonesia, a lower-middle-income country with a population of 260 million, is shifted to the right of the distribution for Ethiopia, a low-income country with a population of 100 million. These pairwise observations reinforce the conclusion reached by Bento and Restuccia (2020) by suggesting that they are robust to market size and sectoral mix.

Looking at the frequency of employment outliers with respect to the sector-year-country average makes it possible to illustrate these patterns even better.[3] Controlling for the structure of the economy as well as for seasonal trends lends support to the main hypothesis: the richer economies under observation, Indonesia and Serbia, consistently report a higher frequency of outliers than the lower-income economies, Côte d'Ivoire and Ethiopia (figure 2.2 for shares of outliers in total number of establishments observed). The premium is robust to different identification methods for outliers.

The approach has limitations. By demeaning with respect to country-sector average and jointly reporting observations from different sectors, the number of outliers for economies where production is highly specialized in a few sectors tends to be lower. Moreover, the number of outliers in each country might not be stable over time: aggregate economic shocks might affect some sectors more than others, and countries with a higher number of firms operating in these sectors could experience noticeable reductions in the number of employment outliers over time. Keeping in mind the rough approximation, the results support the higher probability of encountering large scale of production in richer economies.

Firm characteristics associated with size exhibit similar patterns

Size is not the only feature of firms that stands out in different markets. By focusing only on employment outliers, we might disregard other sources of heterogeneity across firms. For example, establishments reporting a large number of employees might be less productive than smaller ones operating with more advanced technologies. However, given the strong association between size and other firm characteristics illustrated in chapter 1, it is natural to assume similar patterns in the distribution of firm performance across countries at different levels of income. In particular, we would expect productivity differences across firms to be correlated with similar variations in firm size, although less strongly in low- and middle-income economies (García-Santana and Ramos 2015).

The evidence from the two pairs, Côte d'Ivoire–Serbia and Ethiopia–Indonesia, confirms a higher frequency of more productive firms with respect to the sector average in the richer comparator country (figure 2.3). Manufacturing firms operating in Indonesia, for example, are consistently more likely to report higher labor productivity with respect to the sector-year average than Ethiopian firms in the same period.

FIGURE 2.3 Distribution of more productive firms in selected middle- and lower-income countries

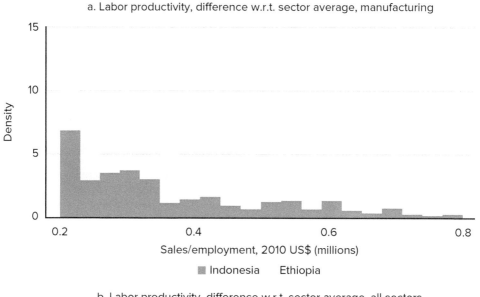

a. Labor productivity, difference w.r.t. sector average, manufacturing

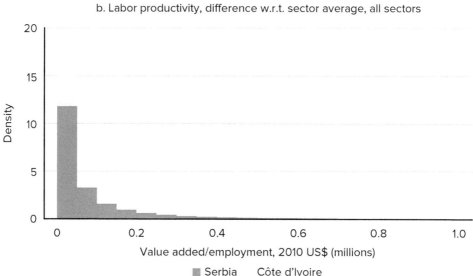

b. Labor productivity, difference w.r.t. sector average, all sectors

Source: Calculations based on business census data for Côte d'Ivoire, Ethiopia, Indonesia, and Serbia
Note: The industrial censuses for Ethiopia and Indonesia only cover the manufacturing sector. w.r.t. = with regard to.

Differences in export revenue along the distribution of firms exhibit similar patterns. Firms reporting export revenues that are higher than the sector average are more present in the richer economy under observation, as suggested by comparisons of the distributions of Côte d'Ivoire–Serbia and Ethiopia-Vietnam (figure 2.4).[4] Overall, differences in establishment size

FIGURE 2.4 Distribution of manufacturing firms reporting export revenue in selected higher- and lower-income countries

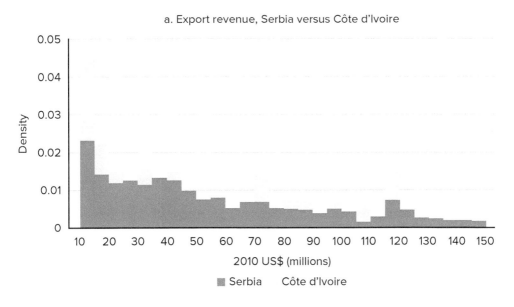

a. Export revenue, Serbia versus Côte d'Ivoire

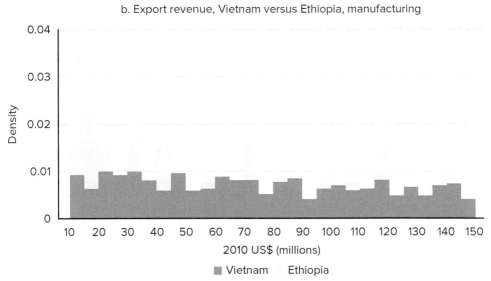

b. Export revenue, Vietnam versus Ethiopia, manufacturing

Source: Calculations based on business census data for Côte d'Ivoire, Ethiopia, Serbia, and Vietnam.
Note: The industrial censuses for Ethiopia and Indonesia only cover the manufacturing sector.

between countries at different stages of development are associated with heterogeneity in firm productivity and export revenue. These findings are robust to considering sectoral differences within countries for the variables of interest.

Employment outliers are different in other related dimensions

Employment outliers tend to stand out in other dimensions as well (table 2.1). For example, they tend to report higher sales and are more likely to be exporters as well as importers of intermediate inputs. Reversing the focus reveals equally strong relationships: productivity outliers, for example, tend to employ a higher number of individuals and are more likely to import or export (see appendix D for detailed results). To give a sense of the differences in scale, a productivity outlier in the sample of the four countries under investigation, on average, employs 98 more individuals than a nonoutlier. The group of exporting firms among productivity outliers is 10 percent larger with respect to nonoutliers. Overall, independent of the characteristics chosen to distinguish performance, the associations remain strong.

Although employment outliers are different than the average firm, they do not simultaneously tend to be export or productivity outliers. The overlap of different types of outliers tends to be below 20 percent in the countries we observe.

TABLE 2.1 Difference in means, employment outliers

Indicator	Employment outlier	Not employment outlier	T-test difference in means
Firm sales, US$ millions	19.922	0.810	19.11***
	(132.92)	(13.013)	182.46
Labor sales productivity	0.053	0.051	0.00218
	(0.270)	(0.681)	1.02
Exporting firms (probability)	0.297	0.106	0.191***
	(0.457)	(0.307)	172.15
Importing firms (probability)	0.517	0.309	0.208***
	(0.500)	(0.462)	69.34
Observations	2,011,065		

Source: Calculations based on business census data for Côte d'Ivoire, Ethiopia, Indonesia, and Serbia.
Note: The industrial censuses for Ethiopia and Indonesia only cover the manufacturing sector. Standard deviations are in parentheses.
*$p < .10$ ** $p < .05$ *** $p < .01$.

Is there a "missing top"?

The "missing middle"—the gap in the middle of the firm-size distribution—is not believed to occur naturally. It is often portrayed as a reflection of market failures associated with development (Hsieh and Olken 2014). In low- and middle-income countries, mid-size firms might be large enough to be regulated and pay higher taxes, yet too small to sustain profit.

Our evidence lends support to an alternative hypothesis in the literature: that the gap is to the right of the firm-size distribution (for exporters, restating the problem as a "truncated top," see Fernandes, Freund, and Pierola 2016; Hsieh and Olken 2014). In other words, the segment that is less likely to be present in low- and middle-income countries consists of large firms rather than mid-size firms. Differences in classifications of large firms might reduce the question to an issue of definition: firms within the range of 50–250 employees may be classified as mid-size firms or as large firms. But the evidence that richer economies in our sample have a greater number of outliers—firms that belong to the extreme of the distribution for employment, labor productivity, and exports—suggests that the larger among the large firms are fewer in number, which warrants further investigation.

What would constitute evidence of a lag in the number of large firms in an economy? The mere shape of the distribution might be informative. Hsieh and Olken (2014), for example, associate the missing middle empirically with evidence of bimodality—distinct peaks (local maximums) at the extremes of the distribution representing very small and very large firms. The observation that relatively less distorted economies have smoother firm-size distributions allows us to examine the hypothesis based on some theoretical shape that fits the rest of the world better. Various alternatives have been suggested: the undistorted cumulative size distribution may be approximated as Pareto (see Axtell 2001; Luttmer 2007; Tybout 2000) or as log-normal (Shimul and Anderson 2019), with arguments in favor of both alternatives (for a review, see Coad 2009).

Use of a Pareto distribution has several advantages: first, its simplicity and widespread use in economics and, second, its close fit with actual firm-size distribution in the United States, often taken as a benchmark case for the lack of market distortions (Axtell 2006). We analyze properties of the employment distribution in each country-year, following Tybout (2014), and repeat the estimations with evidence from less distorted economies in Europe (box 2.1).[5]

Contrary to a nearly perfect match between actual and predicted shares of employment falling under each size category in Europe, the evidence from low- and middle-income countries confirms a sizable gap to the right of the firm-size distribution. The evidence suggests that the larger among the large firms employing more than 300 workers are systematically underrepresented in the lower-income countries under observation. According to our estimates

---

BOX 2.1   A Pareto approximation of the firm-size distribution

If x accounts for the number of workers in each firm, the cumulative distribution of employment in an economy is given by

$$F(x) = 1 - x^{1-k},$$

where the shape parameter of the function, k, accounts for heterogeneities across countries affecting the distribution of employment. Using data on the share of the workforce in different firm-size categories allows us to identify deviations from shares predicted by the Pareto distribution.

When plant size is distributed according to a Pareto function, the share of the labor force employed in plants belonging to size range $l_i \le x < l_j$ is

$$\check{s}\,(l_i, l_j | k) = l_i^{1-k} - l_j^{1-k}.$$

Relying on data from countries in our data set, we can estimate the shape parameter k for each country-year by minimizing the Euclidean distance between the vector of actual shares, s, and the vector of shares predicted by the optimal Pareto distribution, $\check{s}$. We rely on different thresholds to identify firm-size groups.

---

of actual and predicted shares of firms employing fewer than 100 employees, 100–300 employees, and 300 or more employees, the country that is "missing" the largest amount of large firms is Ethiopia, where large firms have a 7 percent lower share of employment than what is predicted by the optimal Pareto distribution (see figure 2.5 for estimates of gaps in different countries).

Assuming the same average characteristics for existing large firms, we can make sense of this number using some counterfactuals on the weight of these missing firms in terms of employment or forgone revenue. Since the median Ethiopian firm in this size category employs more than 500 individuals, the total number of large firms would increase by more than 20 ventures in different manufacturing sectors.[6] If these new large firms were able to obtain revenues equal to the median for firms in this size category, total revenue would rise by US$500 million, leading to a sizable effect on Ethiopia's GDP.[7]

Having a greater number of large firms to match a Pareto distribution would also be beneficial for the richer economies in our group. For example, if Indonesia had the same number of firms as expected, that segment would employ a 4.6 percent higher share of labor, and total manufacturing employment in this country would increase by 237,300 individuals. Since the median Indonesian firm in this size category employs more than 650 individuals, the additional employment would correspond to more than 360 new large ventures of average size.

Two points are worth noting. First, in addition to "missing top" estimates, a gap is also revealed at the lower end of the firm-size distribution. That missing bottom is likely the reflection of an imperfect or censored sampling of small firms, many of which are either excluded from industrial surveys or operate in the informal sector. An imperfect fit of the shape of the Pareto distribution on the left tail could also be behind part of the gap at the bottom. In fact,

FIGURE 2.5   Predicted versus actual share of employment in large firms in selected middle-
and lower-income countries

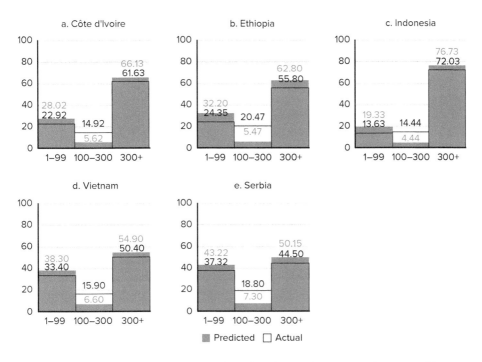

Differences in the actual share minus the predicted share of employment, by country and segment of the
firm-size distribution

Country	Period	k	S < 99 −Ŝ < 99	S < 100–299 −Ŝ < 100–299	S > 300 −Ŝ > 300
Côte d'Ivoire	2003–13	1.07	−0.051	+0.087	−0.045
Ethiopia	2000–11	1.08	−0.078	+0.150	−0.070
Indonesia	2009–15	1.05	−0.057	+0.100	−0.047
Serbia	2006–09	1.12	−0.059	+0.115	−0.056
Vietnam	2007–12	1.11	−0.049	+0.093	−0.045
South Africa	2012 and 2014	1.15	−0.023	+0.042	−0.018

Source: Calculations based on business census data for Côte d'Ivoire, Ethiopia, Indonesia, Serbia, South Africa, and Vietnam.
Note: Median values are reported. The Industrial Censuses for Ethiopia and Indonesia only cover the manufacturing sector.
k = shape parameter of the function (see box 2.1). S = firm size (number of employees).

recent evidence looking at the distribution of productivity across firms in
different countries but also looking at the distribution of employment in the
United States suggests that a convolution of lognormal and Pareto distributions increases precision on the left tail by providing a better fit (see Kondo,
Lewis, and Stella 2018; Nigai 2017). Second, it is noteworthy that the shape
parameters reported in figure 2.5 are not always monotonically and negatively
correlated with per capita GDP, as suggested by earlier work (Coşar, Guner,

and Tybout 2016). Indeed, while results for the pair Ethiopia-Indonesia confirm that the richer country, Indonesia, has a smaller shape parameter, the estimates for Côte d'Ivoire–Serbia suggest that the richer economy has a larger shape parameter.

Modifying the thresholds for robustness lends further support to the hypothesis that the larger among the large firms might be smaller in number in low- and middle-income countries. We distinguish between firms with fewer than 30 employees, with between 30 and 299 employees, and with 300 employees and more. Results suggest that the share of firms employing more than 300 individuals is lower than what is predicted by the Pareto distribution in all countries under observation (see appendix D for details). As previously observed, the country lacking the most large firms is Ethiopia, where, according to the findings, large firms should have had a nearly 10 percent higher share of labor than they actually had in the period 2000–11. The presence of these large of large firms would have been associated with total revenue of more than US$800 million.

Further research to establish patterns of a "missing top" across more countries and to increase their precision would be helpful to validate the evidence presented in this chapter. Additional nuance would be useful, too—for example, examining characteristics and sectoral distributions of firms populating the right tail of the size distribution. Overall, failures preventing smaller as well as mid-size firms from growing could explain these findings.

Perceptions of a "missing middle" have misled policy makers for a long time, with detrimental effects for aggregate growth. The example of India is illustrative in this respect (Freund 2016): convinced that small and medium enterprises drive jobs and growth, in the mid-1970s Indian policy makers restricted about 1,000 manufacturing products to firms in that segment, ultimately forgoing an additional 7 percent increase in jobs as a lower estimate. Firm-size restrictions remained in place until the early 2000s.

Notes

1 | Calculations are based on United States Census Bureau (2016) and OECD (2018).

2 | Based on the World Bank income classification for 2012.

3 | For the purposes of this exercise, we identify as outliers those firms reporting values higher than 1.5 times the interquartile range of the distribution in the respective country-year-sector pair (Tukey Rule).

4 | Due to data constraints, figure 2.4 reports data from exporting firms based in Vietnam instead of Indonesia. Vietnam, in the period 2009–11, belongs to the lower-middle-income group.

5 | In this section we rely on data from Côte d'Ivoire (2003–13), Ethiopia (2000–11), Indonesia (2009–15), Serbia (2006–15), South Africa (2012 and 2014), and Vietnam (2007–12).

6 | We provide this back-of-the-envelope estimate using median total employment by Ethiopian firms employing more than 300 workers during the period under analysis: 56,846.

7 | The median revenue for Ethiopian firms in this size category is equal to US$40 million for the period under analysis.

References

Alfaro, Laura, and Anusha Chari. 2014. "Deregulation, Misallocation, and Size: Evidence from India." BGIE Unit Working Paper 13-056, Harvard Business School, Cambridge, MA.

Alfaro, Laura, Andrew Charlton, and Fabio Kanczuk. 2008. "Plant-Size Distribution and Cross-Country Income Differences." NBER Working Paper 14060, National Bureau of Economic Research, Cambridge, MA.

Axtell, Robert L. 2001. "Zipf Distribution of U.S. Firm Sizes." *Science* 293 (5536): 1818–20.

Axtell, Robert L. 2006. "Firm Sizes: Facts, Formulae, Fables, and Fantasies." CSED Working Paper 44, Center on Social and Economic Dynamics, Brookings Institution, Washington, DC.

Banarji, Ranadev. 1978. "Average Size of Plants in Manufacturing and Capital Intensity. A Cross-Country Analysis by Industry." *Journal of Development Economics* 9 (5): 155–66.

Bento, Pedro, and Diego Restuccia. 2020. "On Average Establishment Size across Sectors and Countries." *Journal of Monetary Economics*, January 14. https://doi.org/10.1016/j.jmoneco.2020.01.001.

Bollard, Albert, Peter J. Klenow, and Huiyu Li. 2014. "Entry Costs Rise with Development." Working Paper 518, Stanford Center for International Development, Stanford University, Stanford, CA.

Coad, Alex. 2009. *The Growth of Firms: A Survey of Theories and Empirical Evidence*. Cheltenham, UK: Edward Elgar.

Coşar, A. Kerem, Nezih Guner, and James Tybout. 2016. "Firm Dynamics, Job Turnover, and Wage Distributions in an Open Economy." *American Economic Review* 106 (3): 625–63.

Fernandes, Ana M., Caroline Freund, and Martha Denisse Pierola. 2016. "Exporter Behavior, Country Size, and Stage of Development: Evidence from the Exporter Dynamics Database." *Journal of Development Economics* 119 (March): 121–37.

Freund, Caroline. 2016. *Rich People Poor Countries: The Rise of Emerging-Market Tycoons and Their Mega Firms*. Washington, DC: Peterson Institute for International Economics.

García-Santana, Manuel, and Roberto Ramos. 2015. "Distortions and the Size Distribution of Plants: Evidence from Cross-Country Data." *SERIEs* 6 (3): 279–312.

Hsieh, Chang-Tai, and Benjamin A. Olken. 2014. "The Missing 'Missing Middle.'" *Journal of Economic Perspectives* 28 (3): 89–108.

Kondo, Illenin, Logan T. Lewis, and Andrea Stella. 2018. "On the U.S. Firm and Establishment Size Distributions." Finance and Economics Discussion Series (FEDS) 2018-075, Board of Governors of the Federal Reserve System, Washington, DC. https://doi.org/10.17016/FEDS.2018.075.

Lewis, W. Arthur. 1954. "Economic Development with Unlimited Supplies of Labor." *Manchester School* 22 (May):139–91.

Liedholm, Carl, and Donald C. Mead. 1987. "Small-Scale Industries in Developing Countries: Empirical Evidence and Policy Implications." Food Security International Development Paper 54062, Department of Agricultural, Food, and Resource Economics, Michigan State University, East Lansing.

Little, I. M. D. 1987. "Small Manufacturing Enterprises in Developing Countries." *World Bank Economic Review* 1 (2): 1–33.

Luttmer, Erzo G. J. 2007. "Selection, Growth, and the Size Distribution of Firms." *Quarterly Journal of Economics* 122 (3): 1103–44.

Nigai, Sergey. 2017. "A Tale of Two Tails: Productivity Distribution and the Gains from Trade." *Journal of International Economics* 104 (January): 44–62.

OECD (Organisation for Economic Co-operation and Development). 2018. "SME and Entrepreneurship Policy in Indonesia 2018." In *OECD Studies on SMEs and Entrepreneurship*. Paris: OECD Publishing.

Poschke, Markus. 2018. "The Firm Size Distribution across Countries and Skill-Biased Change in Entrepreneurial Technology." *American Economic Journal: Macroeconomics* 10 (3): 1–41.

Shimul, Shafiun, and John E. Anderson. 2019. "Missing Middles in Developing Countries: The Role Corruption and Tax Regulation." Paper presented at American Economic Association Annual Meeting, January 4–6, Atlanta. https://www.aeaweb.org/conference/2019/preliminary/1069.

Steel, William F. 1993. "Small Enterprises in Indonesia: Role, Growth, and Strategic Issues." Development of Studies Project 194, BIDE-DAI, Jakarta.

Tybout, James R. 2000. "Manufacturing Firms in Developing Countries: How Well Do They Do, and Why?" *Journal of Economic Literature* 38 (1): 11–44.

Tybout, James R. 2014. "The Missing Middle: Correspondence." *Journal of Economic Perspectives* 28 (4): 235–36.

United States Census Bureau. 2016. County Business Patterns. Retrieved online (May 2020).

3. Large-firm creation: Origins and growth paths

Large firms make important contributions to development, and their numbers in low- and middle-income countries lag behind those in high-income economies. These two facts beg the question of how large firms are created in lower-income contexts and where frictions lie in this process. Turning the focus to the origins and growth paths of large firms is difficult due to the scarcity of evidence. To shed light on this question, we draw on a rare set of industrial censuses from 10 low- and middle-income countries, a comparator data set from 4 high-income Organisation for Economic Co-operation and Development (OECD) economies, as well as records of the origins and sponsors of 1,000 firms that the International Finance Corporation (IFC) has appraised for investment in low- and middle-income countries.

This chapter highlights that what is distinct about large firms is often in place from day one. Large firms are often born large or with features of largeness in their organization, orientation, and capabilities that deviate from the average firm in the industry. Those that grow large from small or medium size pursue growth strategies that are similar to those of large firms from the start, such as product diversification and industrial organization that reflects scale. The evidence highlights the critical role of ex ante differences in firm characteristics, including the intelligence to access and expand demand, in explaining firm growth in low- and middle-income countries, with important implications for policy that are discussed in chapter 4. The growth paths of large firms in low- and middle-income countries are not significantly different from what is observed in high-income economies.

What do we know about the origins of large firms?

Little is known about where large firms originate. The people behind these ventures; their means in terms of intelligence, capital, and capabilities; their strategies; and finally the opportunities they seize have all been identified as successful ingredients of firm growth. All five ingredients—managerial ability, capital, labor, technology, and market access—need to be in place for a new firm to succeed. The features of some of these ingredients are better understood than others; we know more about labor and capital than about managerial talent. Moreover, the exact mix that works in different contexts is less well understood. Is access to technology and the associated lower costs the key to large-firm growth, or is access to markets and demand?

Quantitative cross-country evidence is practically nonexistent, with one exception: the Enterprise Maps, a decade-long effort by the International Growth Centre to trace systematically the history of leading industrial firms in Sub-Saharan Africa (for example, see Sutton 2014; Sutton and Kellow 2010; Sutton and Kpentey 2012; Sutton and Langmead 2013; Sutton and Olomi 2012). Findings of this relatively eccentric strand of literature focus on three aspects of large-firm creation: size at origin, human capital (who started the firms that became large), and the historical circumstances that triggered their creation. One consistent finding is that large firms have often been medium or large at origin. The Enterprise Maps highlight this fact for Ethiopia, Ghana, Mozambique, Tanzania, and Zambia, with several other studies confirming it for other countries (Van Biesebroeck 2005) or for other characteristics associated with size, such as exporting (Freund and Pierola 2015, 2016).

Ownership is another important determinant of size at origin, as firms that start operating at scale from the beginning are often foreign owned (Freund and Pierola 2015, 2016; Sutton 2014)[1] and founded by individuals with extraordinary wealth (Freund 2016) or extraordinary political connections (Rijkers, Freund, and Nucifora 2017). Ownership is associated with advantages in some of the pillars of successful enterprises. Foreign investors, for example, are able to rely on managerial ability, capital, and technology transferred from abroad, while individuals with extraordinary wealth and political connections are often able to secure market access and regulatory protection.

Individuals who create successful firms generally have distinct capabilities. In Sub-Saharan Africa, for example, many large firms were created by managers with trading experience, a seminal finding of the Enterprise Maps project that highlighted the importance of market intelligence and organizational ability for firms to stand out. Knowing what to produce, how to sell it, and how to manage an enterprise effectively might matter more than access to technology in markets that are in the early stages of development. Investors with such abilities—driven by business opportunities, and more educated, motivated, and willing to take risk—are a minority in lower-income countries (Schoar 2010).

These capabilities may often be acquired through former experiences in other activities or firms. Employee spin-offs have been documented as a major mode of entrepreneurship in high-tech manufacturing (Klepper and Sleeper 2005) and a driver of exports (Lafontaine and Shaw 2014; Muendler and Rauch 2018). In the United States, entrepreneurs' prior experience in the specific industry in which they start a new business appears to be highly predictive of their success (Azoulay et al. 2018). Managers and initial workers at high-growth Brazilian firms are reported to be more educated and to have prior experience in managerial occupations or experience in large, formal firms. Nonetheless, these characteristics explain only a small share of variation in firm performance (Bastos, Silva, and Proenca 2018).

Whether firm success is determined by ex ante differences observed at entry or ex post productivity and demand shocks—that is, what happens to the firm after entry—remains an open question. The size of initial investment, and the capabilities of founders and managers at origin, including the technology and market intelligence they bring in, would fall under the category of ex ante differences observed at entry. The origins of large firms matter if we believe that ex ante heterogeneity differences in firm characteristics drive firm success. Recent evidence suggests the magnitude of that influence: in the United States, as much as 40 percent of firm growth 20 years after entry can be attributed to firm differences present at the moment of start-up (Pugsley, Sedlacek, and Sterk 2018).

This discussion is also related to another central question about firm dynamics—that is, the relative importance of efficiency in production versus the demand facing the firm as drivers of firm entry and growth. Theory is divided—some identify heterogeneity in costs of production as the primary source of differences in firm entry and outcomes (Eaton, Kortun, and Kramarz 2011; Hopenhayn 1992; Jovanovic 1989). More recent work highlights demand-side heterogeneity in explaining size differences and market share (Arkolakis 2016; Luttmer 2011). In homogeneous goods industries in the United States, for example, entrants are small and grow slowly despite higher efficiency (Foster, Haltiwanger, and Syverson 2016). In supplier-buyer networks in higher-income economies, differences in appeal to final consumers and downstream intermediate demand rather than cost of production could account for most of the firm-size differences (Bernard et al. 2019; Hottman, Redding, and Weinstein 2016).

Ultimately, the answer to this empirical question will likely vary by context. In Sub-Saharan Africa, findings about the trading origin of industrial firms suggest a dominant role for demand discovery and market creation, while in the Chinese context evidence points toward the substantial contribution of both production cost and demand in explaining sales (Roberts et al. 2018). Historically, it is possible to draw examples to illustrate the role of external shocks such as government interventions or market episodes in large-firm creation. In the late nineteenth and early twentieth centuries, the transition from traders to manufacturers in India, for example, accelerated after a sudden crash in trading profits (Gupta et al. 2018). In Latin America, successful export pioneers have emerged thanks in part to government interventions, as with the flower industry in Colombia or soybean and aircraft production in Brazil (Sabel et al. 2012). These experiences show that experimentation entails high fixed costs and uncertainty. Even when market opportunities have been identified, with missing credit and insurance markets, firms might not be willing to take on such risks without some initial level of demand guarantee or public input provisions.

To sum up, evidence about what distinguishes large successful firms from the rest is only starting to emerge. Theories and empirical evidence exist about the relative role of ex ante heterogeneity versus ex post shocks as well as the importance of supply versus demand in explaining firm-size differences. However, the specific sources of such heterogeneity are less well understood. This chapter adds to this literature by documenting stylized facts across a large sample of firms in low- and middle-income countries: what would be distinct sources of large-firm creation in these geographies, and how do large firms invest, acquire capabilities, and access markets differently over the first few years of operations.

Cross-country information on firm creation

Studying the growth paths of large firms is a data-intensive exercise that needs longitudinal records of firms over several years since their origin. Business registers matched with recurring business censuses are an ideal source of information, but few low- and middle-income countries conduct them systematically and even fewer make the information available for analytical purposes. In addition, some of the fundamental aspects of firm creation such as ownership and management characteristics are typically not recorded in business registers and censuses. Drawing on multiple sources of information is necessary to study the many aspects of firm creation in a meaningful way. This exercise brings together insights from three sources: business censuses from low- and middle-income countries, public records of firms from high-income economies, and a unique set of IFC appraisal documents tracking information on the origins and sponsors of firms evaluated by IFC for possible investment.

A large set of business censuses from low- and middle-income countries

The evidence that follows draws from one of the largest data sets gathered to date to study this question in low- and middle-income countries: firm and establishment longitudinal data from 10 countries.[2] For this analysis, "large" is considered a firm outcome. Therefore, to study the origin of firms, we follow firms that entered at any point in the sample period and managed to survive and become large by the last year (year t) observed. For the growth path analysis, we use all cohorts of firms whose entry as well as survival are observed for at least five years: a total of 18,066 and 26,070 firms in the first and second analyses, respectively.

Cross-country firm-level data have important limitations, one of the most critical being the comparability of employment and capital measures, which can vary from one survey to another. For the purposes of firm origins, the fact that many enterprises do not report figures for employment or economic activity until several years after birth is a major impediment. The misreporting of data at the level of the enterprise is also important. In low- and middle-income countries, misreporting takes place either strategically to ensure compliance with various regulations and incentives or unintentionally due to poor accounting or records kept at the level of the enterprise.[3] There are no readily available ways to verify the accuracy of the individual data; therefore, besides harmonization and some basic imputation, analysis is inevitably constrained by what is available in the surveys or censuses. Country fixed effects, which are used extensively in this analysis, can partly, but not entirely, mitigate systematic biases pertaining to data comparability.

The 10 countries in our sample represent a diverse set of economies with different income levels and growth trajectories. We observe a growing number of large firms in dynamic economies such as China, Ethiopia, Moldova, and Vietnam and a declining trend in countries such as Serbia, where growth has been more anemic during the observed period (figure 3.1). Côte d'Ivoire presents a unique case because it was an economy emerging from civil conflict at the time of observation.

As a comparator group, we use a cohort of more than 31,000 entrants across four countries—France, Italy, Spain, and Sweden—from the OECD DynEmp and Orbis databases to understand how the growth path of large firms might be different in high-income economies. Some limitations exist here as well. While the selection of countries is reassuring in terms of the representativeness of

FIGURE 3.1 Trends in the number of large firms across the sample countries at the start of the year

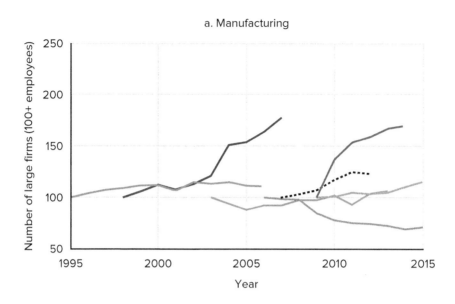

a. Manufacturing

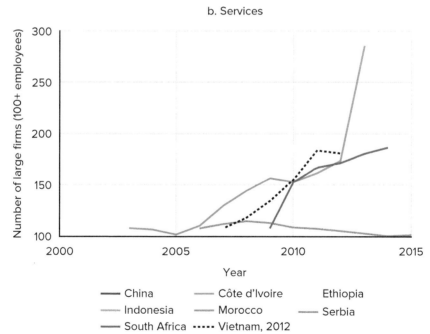

b. Services

Source: Calculations based on industrial census data.
Note: The number of large firms observed in the first year of the survey in each country is normalized to 100. Kosovo and Moldova are plotted separately in appendix G due to the extreme rate of growth in the number of large firms.

large firms, the information for the first year of their operations is often missing. Track records in OECD-Orbis have been commercially sourced from public records with a lag that explains this gap.

A unique set of 1,000 IFC prospective clients tracking information at firm origin

The International Finance Corporation has track records of thousands of prospective clients from low- and middle-income countries that have applied for funding over the last 70 years of its operation. Information on applicants is recorded in a variety of formats and has evolved substantially over the years; it typically includes qualitative descriptions of the origins and growth paths as well the history of sponsors of these firms, as an element for assessing their potential. The data set is a unique source to supplement qualitative information on owners and sponsors that is not available in standard firm-level census data for studying the origins of firms; moreover, it has never been coded systematically to date and has seldom been used for analytical purposes (see appendix E for details of the information that was codified).

This sample comes from manually coding 1,000 appraisal documents for prospective IFC investments between 2015 and 2017, tracking information on firms, their sponsors, and their managers at origin and at the time of investments. The sample covers prospective investment projects from all regions and income levels (see appendix E for details). These firms come in greater numbers mostly from financial (41 percent) and manufacturing (16 percent) sectors with systemic impact.

Selection is the main concern regarding the patterns emerging from this data set. Firms that apply to IFC for funding have a certain international exposure and a certain size that allows them to bear the costs of the process. The selection bias, however, works for the purposes of our study, which focuses on the origins of large, well-managed, productive firms that are missing in low- and middle-income countries. IFC's client selection process screens for these attributes. Yet technically, the pool is not necessarily representative of this category, since many large firms with these attributes do not apply for development finance—either because they can raise capital from other sources, such as retained earnings, or because they do not need as much funding, such as firms in some service sectors.

Ultimately, the key motivation for the study of the sample is that firms that do obtain IFC finance have significant positive impacts on development (by selection) and, in many cases, are of systemic importance for the economy, making their origins of particular interest for the purposes of this study. Also important for the purposes of this study is the fact that most of these large firms have not just begun operations. Their creation spans a much longer period than what recent business censuses provide and makes the sample an exceptionally interesting complement to the information that is publicly or commercially available. Overall, this is a relevant sample for the strategic and policy questions that follow.

Origin of large firms

It is difficult for small firms to grow into large ones

Entrepreneurs driven by business opportunity and growth rather than necessity are a minority in low- and middle-income countries. This established fact is reflected in the unlikely transition of small firms into medium and large firms. Of all firms that enter with fewer than 20 employees and survive for at least five years across our sample countries, close to 89 percent are still small at the end of five years. Only 10 percent of firms grow to become medium size, and 1 percent grow to become large. One might legitimately argue that small shares of transition are due to the short period covered by the evidence. Yet extending the study period to 10 years does not alter the conclusion: the vast majority of firms that start small and survive—83 percent—remain small over that period. Less than 3 percent would grow into a large firm by age 10 (figure 3.2).

FIGURE 3.2   Firm-size transition: Evolution of small firms 5 and 10 years after entry

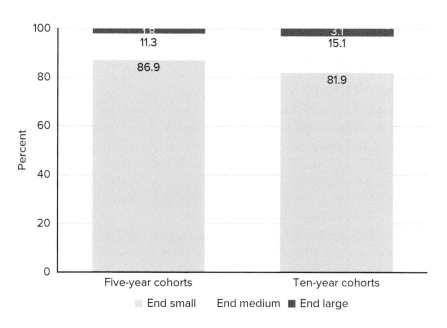

Source: Calculations based on business census data from nine countries (except South Africa; see table 3.1).
Note: Small, medium, and large indicate employment size of 0–19, 20–99, and 100+, respectively.

TABLE 3.1 Description of the sample used in the analysis

Country	GDP per capita (2017, current US$)	Time coverage	Restrictions	Sample 1: large firms in year *t* whose entry we observe	Sample 2: firms that entered and survived at least 5 years	Sample 2: share of firms that started large	Sample 2: share of firms that started small or medium and grew large
China	8,827	1998–2007	Manufacturing firms (legally independent subsidiaries) with sales ≥ 5 million RMB	13,638	4,916	68%	26%
Indonesia	3,847	2010–15	Manufacturing establishments with at least 20 employees (L ≥ 20)	737	449	41%	11%
Vietnam	2,343	2007–12	Full census of large firms, limited information on small firms	3,024	17.310	3%	6%
Moldova	2,290	2004–14	Firms in all sectors	190	658	10%	19%
Kosovo	3,894	2005–14	Firms in all sectors	95	1,953	2%	2%
Serbia	5,900	2006–16	Firms in all sectors, L ≥ 6	145	325	12%	22%
Morocco	3,007	1995–2006	Manufacturing establishments with at least 10 employees (L ≥ 10)	186	262	35%	23%
Côte d'Ivoire	1,662	2003–13	Firms in all sectors	40	178	6%	16%
Ethiopia	768	2000–11	Manufacturing establishments with L ≥ 10 and use powered machinery	11	19	32%	37%
South Africa[a]	6,161	2009–14	Tax records of firms in all sectors				

a. Analyses of South Africa data conducted by the South Africa Treasury, without World Bank direct access to the data.

Large firms, however, are a minority of the business population, so the question of their origin boils down to the share of large firms that were large at origin. Transition rates vary substantially by country and sector, resulting in differences in that indicator (figure 3.3). Many firms, moreover, do not report figures until a year or several years after entry, which adds a margin of error to the estimates of actual size at origin. Overall, in the manufacturing sector of bigger markets—such as China, Indonesia, and Vietnam—the majority of large firms are estimated to be already large at origin. Morocco's high integration into global value chains in both light and heavy manufacturing exposes an otherwise small country to a global market, which likely drives similar patterns (World Bank 2019). In smaller markets—such as Kosovo, Moldova, and Serbia—and in service industries, relatively more firms grow from being a small and medium enterprise (SME) to being a large firm within the same time frame—a distinction that resonates with the loose association between

FIGURE 3.3   Share of five-year-old large firms that were large at origin, by sector

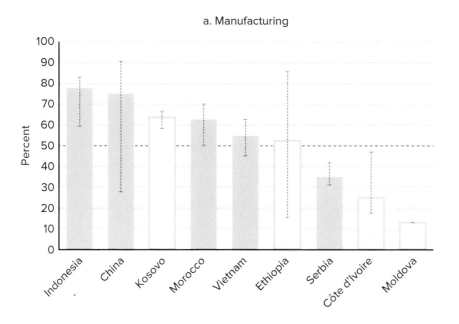

a. Manufacturing

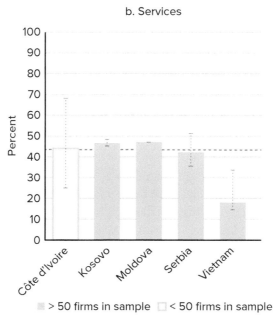

b. Services

■ > 50 firms in sample   □ < 50 firms in sample

Source: Calculations based on business census data from nine countries (except South Africa; see table 3.1).
Note: Empty bars indicate estimates over samples of fewer than 50 firms. The lower estimate corresponds to
the share if all five-year-old large firms with an unobserved origin had started small, and the upper estimate
corresponds to the share if all five-year-old large firms with an unobserved origin had started large. Firms
reporting employment figures within one year from establishment are assumed to have been in the same size
class at origin.

firm size and productivity in services discussed in chapter 1. Extending the growth period to 10 years reduces the available observations considerably but points to similar conclusions: three out of four large firms in China were already large at origin.

In the sample of prospective IFC clients, the pattern is even more pronounced: of all large firms at the time of appraisal, 69 percent were already large at birth. However, a larger share of large firms started as small rather than medium, a clear reflection of the selection of applicants with high growth potential. Selection bias is a major concern, as small firms are underrepresented both in the sample of IFC client companies—a nonrandom sample of the firms with high development impact—and in business censuses, due to various sampling imperfections and informality.

A mix of factors is likely behind these figures. One explanation for cross-country differences in how often large firms are already large at origin is that different starting sizes are feasible across countries, due to the volume of demand, the available technology, or entry barriers. As discussed in chapter 1, these three factors would affect sunk costs at entry or returns to scale, making it unsustainable for firms to enter at small size. Alternatively, in markets plagued by high transaction costs, firms with more complex production might prefer a higher degree of vertical integration and hence start larger. Yet another explanation is financial constraints. If firm size affects the ability to obtain external financing, firms might find it optimal to start larger. It can also be the case that firms start suboptimally small if start-ups are financially constrained. We find suggestive evidence supporting all of these potential explanations (see appendix F, table F.1, for more details).

The sensitivity to these factors is in many ways dependent on the activity of the firm. Service providers, for example, operate typically in less globalized, more customized markets, with less initial capital and high transaction costs for forward linkages. The consistently smaller share of large service providers that were large at origin likely reflects a combination of these drivers. Differences in the availability of technology and market conditions give rise to higher optimal starting size in manufacturing and larger markets, which can partly explain the patterns.

Global patterns across all low- and middle-income countries are hard to obtain due to the scarcity of firm-level data. Patterns across a large number of low- and middle-income countries suggest, however, that at lower levels of development, the share of large firms that begin large at origin is higher (figure 3.4; Bruhn and Xu 2019). About half of large firms surveyed by the World Bank in low-income countries were already large when they started operating.

Rather than it being difficult for firms to *enter* small, another interpretation for these patterns is that it is more difficult for firms to *grow* to scale in some markets.[4] Following cohorts of firms that enter five years before the end of the data sample in each country until the last year (year *t*) allows additional insights

FIGURE 3.4 Share of large firms, by origin size and country income level

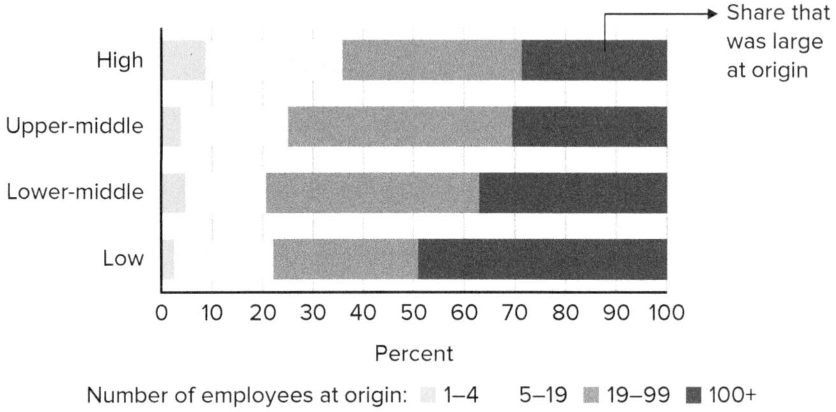

Source: Bruhn and Xu 2019.

in this respect. Following Cabral and Mata (2003), we compare the effect of selection versus growth on the final firm-size distribution by comparing the size distribution of three groups: all entrants in year $t–5$, surviving firms in year $t–5$, and surviving firms in year t (figure 3.4).

The results suggest very different patterns of firm growth and selection across countries for the years considered in the analysis (figure 3.5). For some countries—such as Indonesia, Kosovo, and South Africa—the distribution of firm size changes little five years after firm birth. For Moldova—and, to a lesser extent, Côte d'Ivoire and Morocco—selection at birth explains a significant part of the evolution of the firm-size distribution. In other words, firms are large after five years because survivors are already larger at entry. Surviving firms in Ethiopia are also significantly larger at entry. However, their size distribution flattens out by the end of the sample period, indicating both significant growth and contraction across different sets of firms. In contrast, firm growth appears to explain most of the right shift in the firm-size distribution in China, Serbia, and Vietnam. These results suggest that selection at entry can dominate growth after entry, and vice versa, in different contexts.

The four sources of large-firm creation: foreign investors, the state, domestic investment mobilization, and entrepreneurship

Firms begin with people—sponsors, in investment terms—who use capital, labor, and know-how in order to access a market or create a new one. Who are the sponsors of large firms? Four types of sponsors predominate: foreign firms creating new affiliates, domestic sponsors with experience in other large firms, governments, and entrepreneurs growing smaller ventures to scale. These four actors have different advantages in bringing together the ingredients of successful

FIGURE 3.5 Size distribution of entrants and surviving firms at entry and after five years

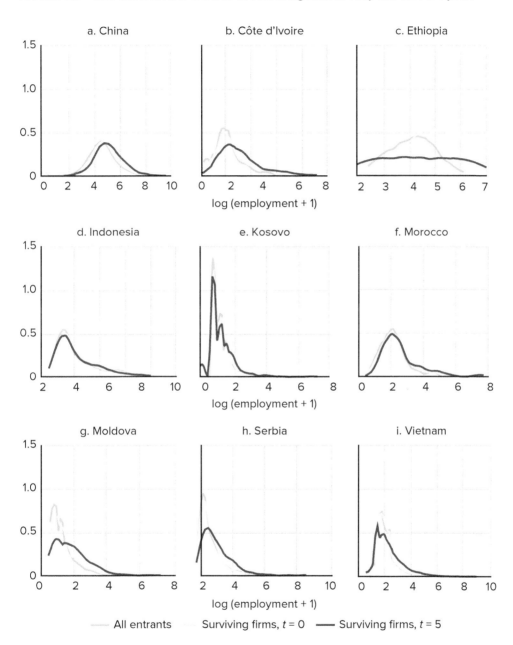

Source: Calculations based on business census data from 10 countries (see table 3.1)

enterprise—capital, labor, technology, managerial talent, and market access. Foreign investors, for example, rely on managerial ability, capital, and technology transferred from abroad for their new ventures. They often enjoy global market intelligence but have to fight for access to local markets. Large domestic firms are often able both to secure market access in new sectors and to transfer know-how,

TABLE 3.2 Foreign ownership at entry and the probability of becoming large

Country	Probability
China	0.196***
Côte d'Ivoire	0.0189*
Ethiopia	0.138
Indonesia	0.366***
Kosovo	−0.000571
Moldova	0.0163***
Serbia	0.111***
Vietnam	0.120***

Source: Calculations based on business census data from eight countries (see table 3.1).
Note: The figures reported are coefficient estimates from regressions of large status (at the end the sample period) on foreign ownership at entry, controlling for sector and entry year fixed effects. Foreign ownership is defined as ownership of more than 10% by foreigners. An exception is China, which is lacking information on shares owned by foreigners. Instead, we rely on a variable that captures the registration type of a firm. Results are qualitatively identical if we also control for initial firm size.
*$p < .10$ ** $p < .05$ *** $p < .01$.

financial capital, and managerial talent from other parts of their business. Smaller entrepreneurs have to acquire know-how through trial and error, face difficulties raising capital from banks and attracting skills, and have limited access to cutting-edge technology. They often rely on innovation and customization to grow.

The prevalence of foreign ownership in larger rather than smaller firms is an established empirical fact. In all country samples, large firms are more likely to have started with some foreign owners than smaller firms. However, the role of foreign ownership at entry appears to vary (table 3.2). In China and Indonesia, foreign ownership significantly increases the probability of large size by close to 37 and 20 percent, respectively. In Côte d'Ivoire and Moldova, this effect is significant but much smaller in magnitude. The result that foreign ownership matters for firm size is in line with knowledge spillovers from foreign direct investment. Why it matters more in certain contexts is less understood.

Beyond foreign ownership, many large firms in former planned economies started off as government ventures and were privatized during transition reforms in the late twentieth century. These ventures have not often created wealth and have suffered from failures in the allocation of resources as well as the lack of incentives to expand until their privatization (Freund 2016). Many relied extensively on foreign know-how to fill gaps in the generation of skills, resources, and know-how to sustain operations, a process that was supported by the state, as in the post-Khrushchev Soviet Union (Hoffmann and Fleron 1980). Ethiopian Airlines illustrates an African state-owned venture that relied on foreign know-how at its very origin, while the government maintained ownership during the company's growth to become one of the leading carriers in Africa (box 3.1). The state origins of large ventures have not been limited to planned economies—in Western Europe and the

---

BOX 3.1 Ethiopian Airlines: A state-owned venture that relied on foreign know-how to grow

After gaining Ethiopia's independence in 1941, Emperor Haile Sellassie reached out to the France, the United Kingdom, and the United States, requesting help to modernize Ethiopia and its economy. The United States responded positively and equipped the nation with materials, promising technical and economic aid to accelerate its development. In that context, a request for technical assistance was made to establish a commercial airline. The United States Department of State arranged meetings between Ethiopian government officials and Brigadier General T. B. Wilson, chairman of the board of Transcontinental and Western Airlines, later known as Trans World Airlines (TWA), who had been directed by the board to expand the airline's operations into foreign countries. An assistance agreement was ultimately signed on September 8, 1945, which committed TWA to establish a commercial aviation company in Ethiopia.

The first chair of Ethiopian Airlines board of directors and president was an Ethiopian and a government minister; the first general manager was an American, H. H. Holloway, appointed by TWA. The carrier, originally called Ethiopian Air Lines, was founded with an initial investment of Br 2.5 million, divided into 25,000 shares that were held entirely by the government. The company was financed by the Ethiopian government but managed by TWA. Consistent with the agreement, TWA management dispatched a team of talented pilots, accountants, administrators, instructors, and technicians to set up Ethiopian Airlines. The Ethiopian government hired TWA to select potential employees, train them, and then assign them in the areas of aircraft maintenance and repair, piloting, and business management. It took almost two decades to meet those objectives; in 1971 the last TWA general manager, Joe Brumit, handed over the office to the first Ethiopian general manager, Semret Medhane. The last TWA contract employee stayed on for an additional three years, until 1974. Since then, Ethiopian Airlines has been fully managed and run by Ethiopian nationals.

Ethiopian Airlines remains 100 percent owned by the government of Ethiopia. Throughout its history, the airline has been one of the pioneers of aviation in Africa and is considered one of the continent's leading carriers today: from its hub in Addis Ababa, Ethiopian Airlines connects passengers to 124 destinations: 20 domestic, 55 in Africa, and 49 others in the Americas, Asia, Europe, and the Middle East. Currently, its fleet includes 87 passenger airplanes, with an additional 61 planes on order.

Sources: Ethiopian Airlines, Star Alliance, and Ethiopian Airlines Former Employees Association.

---

rest of the world, service industries have been dominated by state-owned large ventures for decades, aiming for public provision rather than profits.

Insights on other types of ownership, such as by influential families, are hard to obtain using conventional census data. IFC client data are valuable in this respect because they track detailed profiles of owners to assess the firms' potential. And indeed, except for East Asia, family ownership appears to be significant among larger firms in most regions. The prevalence of family ownership is especially high in South Asia and in Latin America and the Caribbean (figure 3.6). The case of the Tata Group in India illustrates the expansion of a conglomerate, taking advantage of experience in different sectors, while maintaining family ownership throughout its history (box 3.2). Influential families enjoy political connections that often facilitate and protect their ventures from competition, explaining much of their growth.

These large conglomerates are able to transfer know-how, financial capital, and managerial talent from other parts of their business into new ventures.

FIGURE 3.6   Shares of family-owned firms by firm size and region (IFC clients)

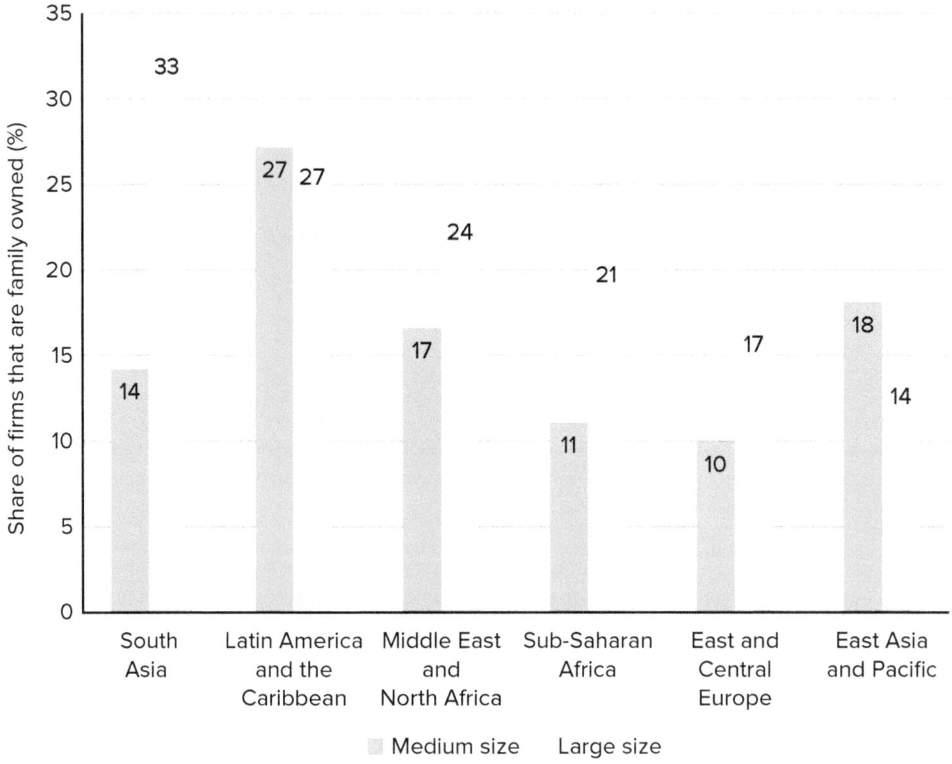

Source: Calculations based on International Finance Corporation proprietary data (2015–17).
Note: IFC = International Finance Corporation.

BOX 3.2   The Tata Group of India: A family-owned conglomerate expanding into different sectors

Jamsetji Tata founded his first trading company, in 1868, at the age of 29. After setting up his company, he bought a bankrupt oil mill at Chinchpokli and converted it into a cotton mill. Within only two years, he was able to turn the mill around and sell it for a profit. He had four goals: (a) set up an iron and steel company, (b) open a unique hotel, (c) establish a world-class learning institution, and (d) establish a hydroelectric plant. However, during his lifetime, he was only able to venture into the hotel business. The Taj Mahal Hotel at the Colaba waterfront was opened in 1903, making it the first hotel with electricity in India. After he died the following year, his older son, Dorabji Tata, became the chairman, following his father's vision by establishing the Tata Iron and Steel Company in 1907. What is today known

as Tata Steel has grown over the last century from its humble beginning to become India's largest integrated private sector steel manufacturer, with a workforce of more than 40,000. It manufactures a wide range of flat and long steel products at its facilities in Jamshedpur. Jamsetji Tata's vision of bringing clean energy to Mumbai by establishing Western India's first hydro plant was also brought to life by his son in 1910—the beginning of Tata Power. The final dream, opening a world-class learning institution, was completed in 1911 with the admittance of the first batch of students to the Indian Institute of Science. The Tata Group debuted its consumer space in 1917, with Tata Oil Mills Company, known for the popular soap brands Hamam and Moti. This business was sold to Hindustan Lever in 1984.

(continued)

BOX 3.2 *Continued*

In the 1930s Tata expanded the group's business into aviation, founding Tata Airlines in 1932. Tata Airlines became a public limited company on July 29, 1946, under the name Air India; after Indian independence in 1947, 49 percent of the airline was acquired by the government of India. The group's rapid expansion continued with the establishment of Tata Chemicals in 1939 and Tata Locomotive and Engineering Company in 1945. Tata discontinued manufacturing steam locomotives in 1971. However, in 1954 the Tata Locomotive and Engineering Company began manufacturing automotive vehicles and officially changed its name to Tata Motors in 2003. The automotive vehicle business commenced with the manufacture of commercial vehicles under financial and technical collaboration with Daimler-Benz AG (now Daimler AG) of Germany. The Tata Group added Tata Global Beverages in 1962 and Tata Consultancy Services in 1968.

A backbone of this expansion has been Tata Administrative Services—an intensive leadership training program that recruits and trains young managers for lifelong mobility across Tata Group companies. Selection takes place within the Tata Group, and the campus selects candidates from the top business schools in India. The aim is to create an exclusive group of managers within the company and provide a rich platform for these talents to realize their full potential in a wide range of industries and functions.

In 2017–18 the revenue of Tata companies, taken together, was US$110.7 billion. These companies collectively employ more than 700,000 people, in a global business group with products and services in more than 15 countries. Each Tata company or enterprise operates independently under the guidance and supervision of its own board of directors. There are 28 publicly listed Tata enterprises with a combined market capitalization of about US$145.3 billion (as of March 31, 2018). Over the years, IFC has partnered with the Tata Group on numerous projects, including a loan agreement with Tata Iron and Steel Company Limited to support Tata Steel's modernization, a partnership to develop strategies to improve water use at some of the group's manufacturing plants, and creation of the first private sector "Green Investment Bank" in India in 2017.

Source: Tata Group.

The case of Tata Administrative Services—the flagship training program that focuses on building transferable management skills across a range of sectors, businesses, and functions of the Tata Group in India—illustrates the mobility that benefits new ventures.

But that is only part of the story. Another explanation for why firms tend to remain family owned while growing very large in low- and middle-income countries is the so-called "principal-agent problem" between the firm's founder and manager. In environments where contracts are harder to enforce, retaining family ownership even as firms reach a larger size might help to overcome the expropriation problem (Burkart, Panunzi, and Shleifer 2003). Yet the literature has also found that family ownership can be detrimental to productivity. One mechanism is through management quality. Lemos and Scur (2018), for example, suggest that family-controlled firms have weaker management practices because they cannot credibly commit to worker discipline. The interplay between the quality of the legal system and structure of firm ownership might be a significant factor limiting firm growth in many parts of the world.

Large firms often build on existing managerial capital

The importance of managerial ability in spurring firm growth has long been acknowledged in the literature. Yet conventional firm-level data contain limited information on the managers of firms (Goswami, Medvedev, and Olafsen 2019). IFC data prove invaluable in that respect. However, echoing the difficulty of identifying the defining characteristics of successful entrepreneurs or the efforts of development institutions to minimize discrimination, there appear to be no discernible differences in the impact of the type of sponsor characteristics—gender, foreign versus domestic, state versus private—on large size among IFC prospective clients.

What stands out is the experience of these companies' managers: almost all firms considered for an IFC investment between 2014–16 have managers with prior experience in the same sector or in another large firm. Of those who also had prior experience in a sector different from the one in which the firm is operating, almost 40 percent came from finance (figure 3.7). There are two possible interpretations of these results. One is that manager experience in finance helps firms to overcome financial constraints. Another is that experience in the financial sector captures general managerial capabilities that are valuable in other sectors.

The example of Secure ID in Nigeria, an IFC client, showcases the advantage that employee spin-offs have in intelligence about their parents' markets—that is, knowledge about demand rather than supply (box 3.3). The experience of Tbilvino in Georgia is reminiscent of the observation that "successful industrializers got out early and often"—in other words, the importance of learning from foreign technologies and markets (Cusolito and Maloney 2018), but also the critical role of managerial ability for firm resilience in the face of demand shocks (box 3.4).

FIGURE 3.7 Experience of managers of prospective IFC client companies

Current size	Manager had experience from same sector	Manager had prior experience in large firms
Large	98%	93%
Medium	100%	93%
Small	100%	92%

In which other sectors does the manager have experience?

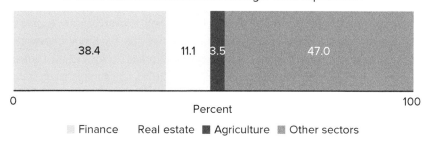

Finance   Real estate   Agriculture   Other sectors

Source: Calculations based on International Finance Corporation proprietary data (2015–17).
Note: IFC = International Finance Corporation.

BOX 3.3   Secure ID, Nigeria: Entrepreneurship building on large-firm experience

Established by Kofo Akingkube in 2005, Secure ID is the largest supplier of bank smartcards and other security-sensitive cards in Nigeria as well as the first certified smartcard manufacturing plant in Sub-Saharan Africa. After serving in the Nigerian Youth Service Corps, Akingkube started her career in the banking industry, working with International Merchant Bank Plc and Chartered Bank Limited. She remained in the financial sector for more than 12 years, until 1997, when she left to start Interface Technologies Ltd. (ITL), a security management and biometrics technology company. With a bachelor's degree in mathematics and a master's degree in business administration from the University of Strathclyde, she successfully ran ITL for nine years, before establishing Secure ID Nigeria Ltd., an offshoot from a small department of ITL and the first VISA-certified plant in Sub-Saharan Africa.

Today, Secure ID is Nigeria's leading smartcard manufacturing and personalization plant, providing comprehensive end-to-end payment services, while identifying management and digital security solutions for the financial services sector, telecommunications, government, education, health care, and private enterprises. The company is fully certified by VISA, Verve, and MasterCard and operates a world-class production plant employing best practices and international standards. The company's client base spans five African countries and is the leading EMV-certified card plant in West Africa, one of six in Africa, and a member of the elite club of only 80 such companies in the world. Located in the heart of Lagos, Secure ID is fully certified by the requisite global industry organizations, and it currently has an installed capacity for producing 200 million cards per year, with scope for future expansion. Secure ID's success has been setting the standard for innovation and creativity in the smartcard sector in Sub-Saharan Africa.

An International Finance Corporation equity investment in 2015 of up to US$6 million in Secure ID supports the development of non-oil sectors with strong export potential and also supports small and medium enterprises' access to finance in Sub-Saharan Africa.

BOX 3.4   Tbilvino, Georgia: The importance of managerial ability for resilience and growth

The story of Tbilvino begins in 1962, when one of the most powerful wine factories in the Soviet Union was launched. That was also the year when Tbilisi held its 10th International Congress of Winegrowers. For years, the factory remained a significant part of the Soviet wine-making industry, with 9 of every 10 bottles of wine sold inside the country and abroad being made in this factory. In the early 1990s, it emerged as an independent wine company with a new philosophy and approaches; the company is still undergoing substantial development, both in its infrastructure and in the growing sophistication of its wines.

Brothers Zura and Giorgi Margvelashvili were shareholders in Tbilvino, post-1991. After Zura returned from a wine-making internship in California, he was inspired to work with wine, and the brothers invested the family savings in a share buyout, taking control of Tbilvino in 1998. When they took over the business, as Giorgi recalls, "Tbilvino was not in very good shape in 1998—it had close to zero production. Contact with former suppliers and customers was lost." The brothers built Tbilvino up from this unpromising start, with a radically different approach from the Soviet process of blindly accepting and bottling bulk wine. The new strategy meant getting involved with the many growers who supplied the grapes, taking an active part in the harvest, and upgrading the quality of the wine.

In 2006 the company lost around 52 percent of its business when a Russian import embargo on Georgian wine kicked in. The shock was an opportunity for change. Most of the Tbilisi site was sold off to raise money, and a new, smaller, quality-optimized winery was built, focusing on exports to the European market. Finally, by 2008, Tbilvino had recovered, stronger than ever, under the Margvelashvili brothers' leadership. Today the company produces around 4 million bottles a year and exports to 30 countries,

(continued)

BOX 3.4 *Continued*

producing as many as 18 million bottles a year in its heyday. Currently, as a joint stock company with 105 employees, Tbilvino is the largest Georgian wine exporter by volume and procures grapes from more than 300 small farmers located in the Kakheti region. In 2015 the International Finance Corporation provided a US$1.5 million loan to support Tbilvino's investment in crushing and processing equipment, with the aim of spurring job creation and generating tax revenues for the state budget in Georgia.

Growth paths of large firms

Many large firms start off large and build on existing managerial capital and assets. But what about the minority of firms that grow large from smaller sizes? Are their strategies in any way aligned with those of firms born large? This section examines the question by comparing the growth path of firms starting at different sizes over several key outcomes such as employment, labor productivity, exports, and financing over their life cycle.[5] Track records of firms allow only observations for five years after they enter.[6] These first years of a firm's life cycle capture important dynamics given the overall high rate of firm exits. In low- and middle-income countries, more than 95 percent of firms that start off with fewer than 10 employees disappear within that time frame (Merotto, Weber, and Aterido 2018). Even in mature economies such as the United States, half of start-ups fail within that period (Pugsley, Sedlacek, and Sterk 2018).

More formally, the growth paths of firm outcomes can be captured in a simple framework using an interaction between indicators of firm-size group and years after entry in the following specification: $y_{ics} = \beta \times sizegroup_i \cdot d_t + \alpha_{cs} + d_{it0} + \varepsilon_{ics}$, where y_{ics} indicates the firm outcome, $sizegroup_i$ indicates the size group the firm belongs to, α_{cs} indicates country x sector fixed effect, d_{it0} the cohort-start year fixed effect, and ε_{its} the error term

To account for differences that might be driven by country characteristics, sector composition, and macroeconomic trends, the regressions also control for country-sector fixed effects and cohort fixed effects. The spotlight is on four types of large firms: firms that started large, firms that started small or medium but grew large within five years, and other surviving and nonsurviving firms.[7]

This simple descriptive exercise brings a wealth of insights on how large firms enter, access markets, make investments, and acquire capabilities differently as they grow. In what follows, we discuss these results in four main areas: (a) firm size, (b) role of efficiency versus demand for entry and growth, (c) investment in capabilities, and (d) role of organizational capital.

Firms that start large retain a substantial size and productivity premium

Across countries, on average, firms that grow large are substantially smaller than firms that were large at entry (see figure 3.8 for the predicted employment and confidence interval by size group at each year after firm's entry).[8] However, these smaller, high-growth firms expand rapidly in the first year and by the fifth year after entry more than halve the employment gap with firms that start large. Large firms that start large also grow, albeit more slowly. Average employment for the rest of the firms stays flat throughout the observed period.

Sales follow a trajectory similar to employment across smaller, high-growth firms and large firms, with one major difference: firms that are large at origin also attain, on average, significant sales growth after entry. At age five, the levels of output of these firms are about 2.5 times higher than at entry. The contrast between rapid growth of some firms over others is consistent both across and within countries, suggestive of a "winner takes all" environment. These high-growth firms are transformational in ways that have been discussed extensively in the literature (Schoar 2010).

Growth differences are reflected equally in firm productivity: those that start off large or grow large are more productive. All firms attain some productivity growth by the fourth to fifth year of age, with the average value added per worker being similar for large firms independent of their start size and significantly higher than that of firms that stay small or exit. As expected, substantial productivity gaps persist between surviving firms and exiting firms, especially at the year prior to exit. However, conditional on survival, there is little evidence of selection on labor productivity at entry and in the first three years of a firm's operations.

The labor productivity growth path is unique in that it is the only characteristic that seems statistically similar in the first two to three years for these different firm-size groups (figure 3.9). What can explain the similarity in observed labor productivity over the early years of firms' operations? Short-lived demand could explain the early growth of all types of firms. The pattern stresses the importance of expanding demand—either through exports or through product diversification—for a firm's survival and transition to larger scale.

Market access distinguishes firms that start or grow large from the rest

Large firms are increasingly likely to export over time. At entry, SMEs exhibit similar export propensity independent of their later outcomes. That propensity is low, in contrast to the propensity of firms that start off large. However, firms that grow large narrow the exporting gap quickly after entry—by age five, about

FIGURE 3.8   Growth paths in employment and sales

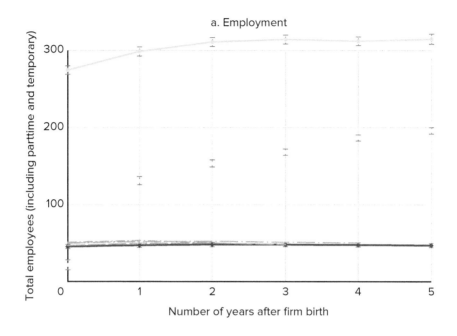

a. Employment

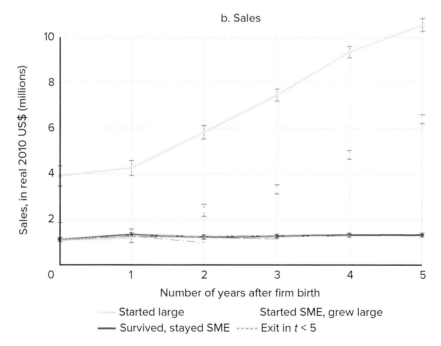

b. Sales

— Started large   Started SME, grew large
— Survived, stayed SME   ····· Exit in $t < 5$

Source: Calculations based on business census data from 10 countries (see table 3.1).
Note: Small, medium, and large indicate employment size of 0–19, 20–99, and 100+, respectively.
Predicted values and 95% confidence interval from regressions of employment on size group*years after
entry, controlling for country*two-digit sector fixed effects as well as cohort start-year dummies. Firm
employment is winsorized at the 1% tails at the country level. SME = small and medium enterprise.

FIGURE 3.9   Growth path in labor productivity

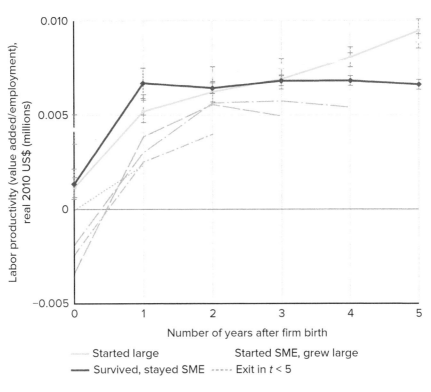

Source: Calculations based on business census data from 10 countries (see table 3.1).
Note: Small, medium, and large indicate employment size of 0–19, 20–99, and 100+, respectively. Predicted values and 95% confidence interval from regressions of employment on size group*years after entry, controlling for country*two-digit sector fixed effects as well as cohort start-year dummies. Firm employment is winsorized at the 1% tails at the country level. SME = small and medium enterprise.

30 percent of both types are exporting directly. SMEs that do not survive do not have significant differences in their exporting status (figure 3.10). Large firms in which IFC invests exhibit a similarly pronounced export orientation and are more likely to report foreign expansion as their growth strategy (figure 3.11).

These paths are not surprising: only firms beyond a certain size and productivity level can afford the fixed cost of exporting (Melitz 2003). Hence, while all firms seem to increase labor productivity over time, large firms are increasingly likely to export while others remain nonexporters. What is surprising is that high-growth firms close the exporting gap so quickly or that a nonnegligible share of firms already export at entry, given the arduous process of learning that the activity involves. The accumulation of capacities and linkage needed for export production—a process of simultaneously exploring what should be made and how to make it—often takes years (Sabel et al. 2012). This result could be a data artefact if these firms are spin-offs from more established firms. It could also be the case that these entrepreneurs have already identified some prior demand

FIGURE 3.10   Growth paths: Exporting and product diversification

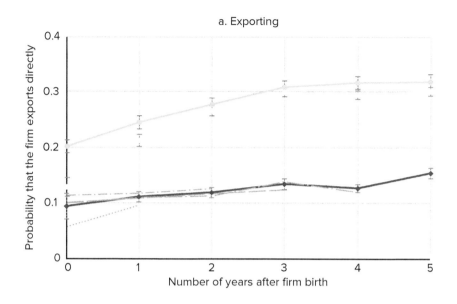

a. Exporting

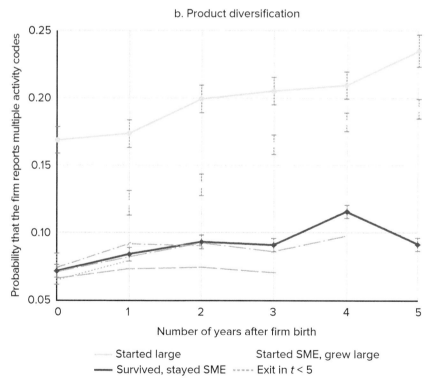

b. Product diversification

Started large   Started SME, grew large
—— Survived, stayed SME   ----- Exit in *t* < 5

Source: Calculations based on business census data from 10 countries (see table 3.1).
Note: Small, medium, and large indicate employment size of 0–19, 20–99, and 100+, respectively. Predicted values and 95% confidence interval from regressions of employment on size group*years after entry, controlling for country*two-digit sector fixed effects as well as cohort start-year dummies. Firm employment is winsorized at the 1% tails at the country level SME = small and medium enterprise.

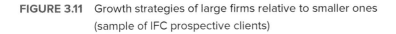

FIGURE 3.11   Growth strategies of large firms relative to smaller ones
(sample of IFC prospective clients)

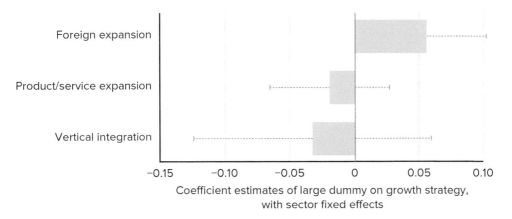

Coefficient estimates of large dummy on growth strategy,
with sector fixed effects

Source: Calculations based on International Finance Corporation (IFC) proprietary data.
Note: Coefficient estimates and 95% confidence interval of large-firm dummy on stated growth strategy, with sector fixed effects. Results are less precise but almost identical when excluding the financial sector.

and enter the market to satisfy that demand, as when employee spin-offs export to their parent-firm markets (Muendler and Rauch 2018). The fact that traders accumulate knowledge about demand that, in turn, drives their success in industrial activities has been highlighted in the Enterprise Maps (Sutton 2014; Sutton and Kellow 2010; Sutton and Kpentey 2012; Sutton and Langmead 2013; Sutton and Olomi 2012). Finally, as noted in a now extensive literature, conventional measures of productivity suffer from difficulties in separating physical efficiency and demand from typical firm-level data (Cusolito and Maloney 2018). As such, the observed trends in increasing labor productivity and exporting can also be driven by the fact that firm growth is driven by rising demand.

New sources of demand spur firm growth, whether it be in different countries or in different products and services. Operating in multiple industries over time—a proxy for product diversification—falls into that category of drivers and illustrates growth strategies with similar paths to exporting. Large firms that enter large are the most diversified, with 16 percent and 24 percent of them operating in multiple industries at entry and five years after entry, respectively. Almost all firms that started at smaller sizes operate within one industry at entry. By age five, however, close to 20 percent of firms that grow large have diversified into at least one more industry. Surviving SMEs also diversify over time, albeit at a much lower rate relative to those that grow large, and exiting firms do not diversify for the most part. These results highlight the importance of market access and the associated intelligence as a driver of firm size at entry and growth over time.

BOX 3.5   Wadi Group, Egypt: Product and market diversification as a growth strategy

Launched in Egypt in 1984 with a small-scale poultry operation, today Wadi Group operates in 12 subsidiaries with 10 brands in three distinct sectors. The chairman of the board of directors and shareholder, Musa Suleiman Freiji, is a leading figure in the Middle Eastern poultry industry, with experience spanning 50 years in Egypt, Jordan, Lebanon, Saudi Arabia, and the Syrian Arab Republic. His commercial experience in the poultry industry dates from 1957 when he became the production manager at Greenleaf Poultry Company in Zahle, Lebanon. Thereafter, he established and managed 13 poultry and poultry-related operations in the Arab world, seven of which are still operational.

Although the company's activities were historically concentrated in poultry, Wadi has expanded its business since 2004, diversifying into production of primary agricultural products (for example, olives, grapes, and vegetables), food processing, commercial poultry feed, cell pads, logistics, and glass containers. Geographically, Wadi has also expanded its poultry business in Sudan and currently has a

market share close to 50 percent in the day-old broiler chicken market there. With more than 3,250 employees, Wadi has played a significant role in creating direct and indirect jobs by making the company's funding sources more sustainable. Meanwhile, the synergy that Wadi Group has developed between its various sectors has been crucial to improving efficiency and ensuring sustainability. The company has also contributed to turning the desert green, helping to make poultry an affordable household staple, and has successfully integrated industry across the supply chain, while also playing an instrumental role in ensuring that grain-handling logistics are as safe and efficient as possible. The International Finance Corporation's US$22 million loan in 2017 supports Wadi Group efforts to expand its exports, which will help to generate foreign currency in Egypt. In addition, this investment aims to increase the reach of farmers and small and medium enterprises as the company enters new product markets and expands the company's economic reach through distributors and suppliers.

Source: International Finance Corporation.

The cases of Wadi Group in the Arab Republic of Egypt (described in box 3.5) and the Indonesia-based Indorama Group (described in box 3.6), both IFC clients, illustrate the importance of product diversification and foreign market access as a growth strategy for firms in low- and middle-income countries.

Firm size goes hand-in-hand with investment in capabilities

Large firms build on existing human capital through the experience of their founders or managers. At the same time, investment in skills is a distinct growth strategy to maintain comparative advantage over time.

One proxy for the quality of human capital is wages. Wage growth over time mirrors labor productivity growth for most firms: average wages increase generally with firm age for all size groups (figure 3.12). Notably, large firms that enter at smaller sizes pay similar wages at entry as those that start large and increase their wages at a similar rate. The wage gaps between large firms, surviving SMEs, and exiting firms are more clear-cut. At entry and five years after entry, the average wages of large firms are significantly higher than those of SMEs. Despite similar

BOX 3.6   Indorama Group, Indonesia: The importance of foreign expansion for growth in the chemical industry

Founded by Sri Prakash Lohia and his father as Indorama Synthetics in 1976, Indonesia-based Indorama Group is currently the largest global producer of polyethylene terephthalate (PET) as well as the second largest manufacturer of olefins and polyolefins in Africa, with manufacturing facilities in six sites, including Indonesia, Thailand, and Uzbekistan. S. P. Lohia was born in India in 1956, but moved with his family to Indonesia in 1973. His father, who already had a small garment business, inspired him to start Indorama Synthetics in 1976. At first, the company only produced synthetic yarn, but later he and his brother Anil Prakash started to expand their product line to polyester fiber and PET (bottle-grade polyester). In 1995 the company started to produce resin products, and profits began to rise significantly.

In 2006 S. P. Lohia set up base in Africa and invested in the fledgling petrochemical industry by acquiring Nigeria-based Eleme Petrochemicals Company. Under his leadership, Indorama Corporation is now the largest foreign investor in West Africa's petrochemicals sector and so far has invested close to US$2 billion in the region. From one small company, the business later expanded to Indorama Shebin, ISIN Lanka, and Indorama

IPLIK; all of these companies produce products related to synthetic fiber, such as polypropylene, PET resin, and polyethylene. Later, he also built Medisa Technologies, which made medical gloves. The Indorama Group has grown from US$10 million to almost US$10 billion over the last 40 years, operating in as many as 19 countries, with 10,000 employees in Indonesia and more than 30,000 employees worldwide. Indorama Group not only has spurred job creation all over the world, but also has played an instrumental role in international trading and brought increasing revenues to Indonesia.

In 2014 an International Finance Corporation loan of nearly US$40 million to Indorama Kokand Textile in Uzbekistan provided support for 900 permanent jobs in a local market, of which more than 80 percent are women employees, primarily in underdeveloped areas of Uzbekistan. The expansion of business to Uzbekistan also supported significant south-south investment in a country that has had difficulty attracting foreign direct investment, while also contributing directly to increased export of higher-value-added products in a priority sector for the country, within seven years.

Source: International Finance Corporation.

levels of productivity at entry, persisting gaps suggest that large firms have higher-quality workers at entry. This finding is consistent with studies discussed earlier, such as Bastos, Silva, and Proenca (2018), and with evidence from chapter 1 that large firms employ disproportionally more educated workers.

"Physical" capabilities exhibit similar patterns, as illustrated by the growth of investments in assets and inputs over the first years of a firm's life cycle. Not surprising, large firms have a significantly higher stock of capital (fixed assets) at entry and beyond.[9] SMEs that grow large have lower initial capital stock, on average, but they gradually catch up with firms that are born large. The trend in capital stock implies consistent capital investment over time by large firms that are born smaller, in excess of investments by those that are born large. In contrast, other SMEs and exiting firms make, on average, negligible investment in fixed assets.

The pattern in a range of measures of intangible investments and input use is less clear. No discernible pattern arises in large firms versus SMEs in the use

FIGURE 3.12   Growth path in wages

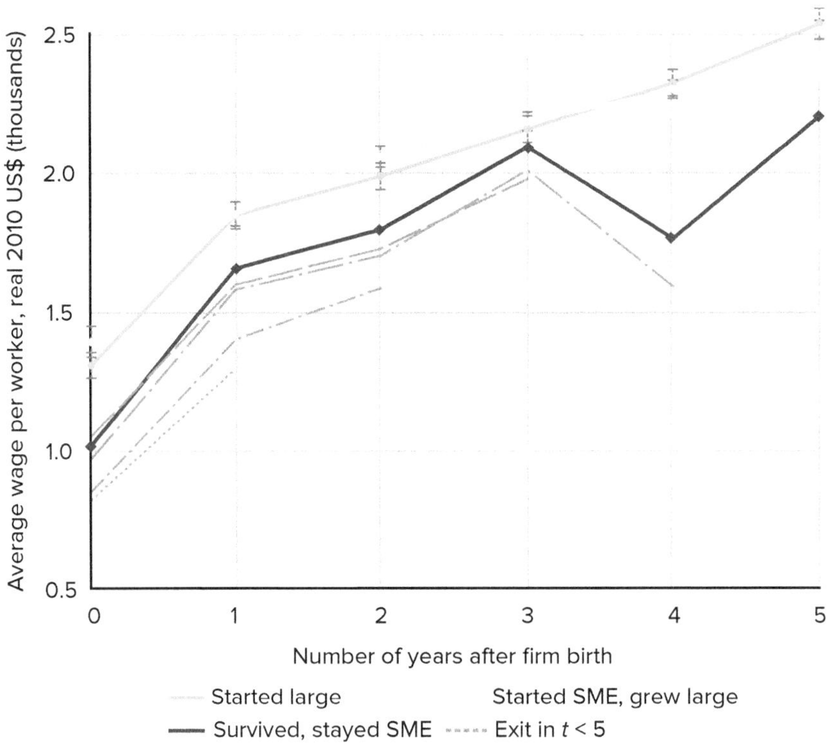

Source: Calculations based on business census data from 10 countries (see table 3.1).
Note: Small, medium, and large indicate employment size of 0–19, 20–99, and 100+, respectively.
Predicted values and 95% confidence intervals from regressions of employment on size group*years
after entry, controlling for country*two-digit sector fixed effects as well as cohort start-year dummies.
Firm employment is winsorized at the 1% tails at the country level. SME = small and medium enterprise.

of imported inputs, in service inputs over sales or investments in research and development, or in the share of firms' intangible assets over total assets. The lack of statistical evidence about differences in input use and investment in intangible capital is partially due to limited sample size, since these variables are only recorded in a small subset or a single country in our sample. But it also suggests that other dimensions of firm capabilities are not well measured in existing data (for an overview of difficulties in measuring intangibles, see Haskel and Westlake 2017, for example). More generally, many important determinants of a firm's capabilities such as knowledge, use of specific technologies, and other inputs are rarely captured in existing firm-level data sets (Bloom et al. 2014).

Differences in the pattern of capital accumulation can be instructive about firm constraints. Unlike firms that grow large, there are no discernible changes in the level of capital stock by firms that enter large (figure 3.13). It is possible that SMEs enter at a smaller scale due to uncertainty about demand or

FIGURE 3.13   Growth path in capital stock and investment

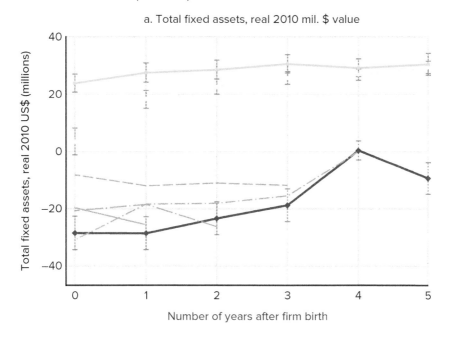

a. Total fixed assets, real 2010 mil. $ value

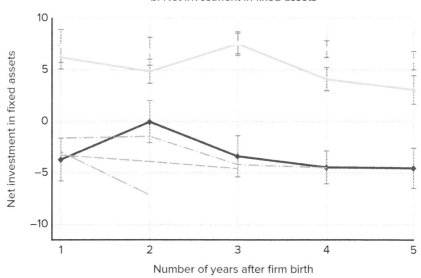

b. Net investment in fixed assets

Regression includes country FE*2–digit sector FE as well as cohort start year dummies.

——— Started large   Started SME, grew large
——— Survived, stayed SME   ----- Exit in *t* < 5

Source: Calculations based on business census data from nine countries (see table 3.1).
Note: Small, medium, and large indicate employment size of 0–19, 20–99, and 100+, respectively. Predicted values and 95% confidence interval from regressions of total fixed assets and investment in fixed assets on size group*years after entry, controlling for country*two-digit sector fixed effects as well as cohort start-year dummies. Firm outcome is winsorized at the 1% tails at the country level. Results include China, Côte d'Ivoire, Moldova, and Vietnam only due to data availability. SME = small and medium enterprise.

productivity and only make gradual investments as they acquire market intelligence. It might also be the case that SMEs face financial constraints and can only scale up investments as they grow. Little evidence exists to distinguish these two hypotheses.

To what extent do firms of different sizes rely on external finance to grow? Firms that start large are able to secure finance from the first day of their operations, possibly capitalizing on the experience of their founders and managers, but also on the volume of commitment at the beginning. High-growth firms starting at smaller sizes need to prove their potential and creditworthiness before acquiring external finance. Compared to firms that start off large, they have significantly less leverage at entry—that is, they have significantly less external debt relative to their total assets (figure 3.14). The gap in leverage narrows significantly and disappears by age five. Large firms among IFC clients also disproportionately report reinvested earnings as a source of financing, suggesting that they capitalize on existing resources in addition to external sources of financing for growth (figure 3.15). The evidence could well reflect financial constraints, likely overstating the use of internal finance in large firms that are not soliciting funds from development finance institutions.

FIGURE 3.14 Growth path in leverage (ratio of total liabilities to total assets)

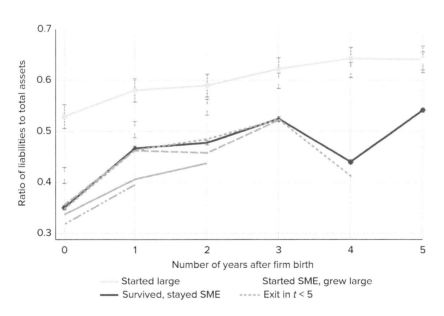

Source: Calculations based on business census data from nine countries (see table 3.1).
Note: Small, medium, and large indicate employment size of 0–19, 20–99, and 100+, respectively. Predicted values and 95% confidence interval from regressions of leverage on size group*years after entry, controlling for country*two-digit sector fixed effects as well as cohort start-year dummies. Firm outcome is winsorized at the 1% tails at the country level. Results only include Côte d'Ivoire, Moldova, and Vietnam due to data availability. SME = small and medium enterprise.

FIGURE 3.15   Financing strategies of large firms relative to smaller ones (sample of IFC prospective clients)

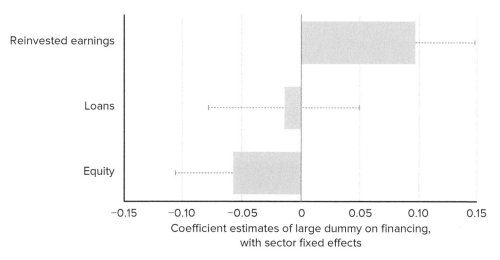

Source: Calculations based on International Finance Corporation (IFC) proprietary data.
Note: Coefficient estimates and 95% confidence interval of large-firm dummy on stated growth strategy, with sector fixed effects. Results are less precise, but almost identical when excluding the financial sector.

BOX 3.7   Atasu Logistics, Kazakhstan: Moving from internal to external finance for growth

Atasu is an Almaty-headquartered private company specialized in providing logistics solutions in Kazakhstan and the region, with the focus on serving import and transit cargo from China. In 1998, at the age of 22, Marat Zhuman, a Kazakh national, founded Atasu Logistics. Using reinvested earnings, he grew the company organically from a small asset-light freight-forwarding business to a well-established entity employing more than 350 people. Atasu has recently completed an equity financing deal with the CITIC Capital Silk Road Fund, which joins the company as a significant minority shareholder. In addition, the company has raised financing from the European Bank for Reconstruction and Development and plans to direct the funds to develop the company in the logistics industry and to strengthen its position in the international market.

Source: International Finance Corporation.

Yet sources of finance are never mutually exclusive. Rather the opposite: a higher level of commitment typically mobilizes a greater volume of external finance in a mix that likely evolves over time. The case of Atasu Logistics, an IFC client, illustrates the evolution in the mix of reinvested earnings as a source of finance for growth early on, gradually reaching the equity markets as the firm matures (box 3.7).

SMEs that grow large organize production differently
from the beginning

The organization of production through "layers" of employment—or knowledge-based hierarchies—has been highlighted as an essential mechanism for firm growth. In fact, growth is often seen as an endogenous process of accumulating organizational capital—in other words, information—but early discussions have been silent about the specific mechanisms in place (Luttmer 2011; Prescott and Visscher 1980). The allocation of workers into hierarchical layers allows the firm to minimize cost, which could be a motivation for firms to reorganize as they grow (Luttmer 2011; Prescott and Visscher 1980). Reorganization matters because it economizes on the knowledge of all preexisting layers.[10]

Little information is available to assess firms' evolution in that respect in low- and middle-income countries. For this study, we rely on the case of Côte d'Ivoire, where the census data allow us to disaggregate employment and define layers based on hierarchical occupational categories.[11] As expected, the evidence shows a distinct employment structure that includes more layers for firms that start large and grow large, even at the moment of entry (figure 3.16). The number of layers in SMEs that grow large is statistically higher than in other SMEs and is similar to firms that start off large. The average number of layers also tends to increase for large firms over time. The same pattern holds with alternative measures of internal organization, such as whether firms have all employment layers or whether they have the top layer.

This result suggests that organizational capital and the ability to reorganize might be a critical asset for successful firms. When viewed together with the supply side of skills, this result is also informative of the constraints that might prevent firms from growing large. After all, the firm's span of control is affected by the skills composition in the labor market (Eeckhout and Kircher 2018). Depending on the skills' distribution in the economy, better (high-productivity) firms might be smaller even without any market distortions.

The growth of large firms is not much different in
high-income countries

A lot of what is different about large firms in high-income countries is driven by frontier firms: conglomerates that dominate global markets and push the productivity frontier of multiple industrial countries at once. With few exceptions, these firms are not young; they operate one way or another for decades and grow from a large base.

The growth path of firms over the first years of their life cycle illustrates a process typically taking place away from the frontier. Some of the fundamental aspects of firms' growth, such as the importance of market access and

FIGURE 3.16   Growth path in organizational capital (proxied by employment layers)

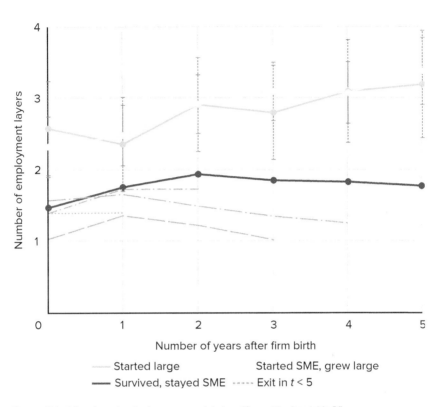

Source: Calculations based on business census data from 10 countries (see table 3.1).
Note: Small, medium, and large indicate employment size of 0–19, 20–99, and 100+, respectively.
Predicted values and 95% confidence intervals from regressions of employment on size group*years
after entry, controlling for country*two-digit sector fixed effects as well as cohort start-year dummies.
Firm employment is winsorized at the 1% tails at the country level. SME = small and medium enterprise.

investment in capabilities, are therefore not expected to be different. What would be expected, however, is a sharper growth path given the absence of several market distortions that hamper firm growth at entry in low- and middle-income countries.

Results from a cohort of more than 30,000 large firms in the OECD DynEmp and Orbis databases confirm this basic intuition, with growth paths being, on average, similar to observations in low- and middle-income countries yet sharper in the trends they illustrate (see appendix H for illustrations of growth paths in France in terms of employment, sales, labor productivity, capital stock, investment, and wages). Firms that start off large retain a significant premium in size, sales, export propensity, and investment over the first years of their operations, while firms that grow large record rapid expansion of investment and foreign market access. However slim, this comparator evidence highlights commonalities in the early process of firm growth and capitalization of capabilities across different income contexts.

To summarize, the patterns of firms' origins and growth paths highlighted in this chapter resemble a so-called "separating equilibrium" whereby large firms have characteristics and make decisions that distinguish them from the rest. The minority of SMEs that grow large narrow the gaps quickly and follow often similar strategies reflecting scale from the beginning.

How do we interpret these results in light of theories of firms' growth? The distinct growth path of large firms seems to suggest that ex ante differences in capabilities, including intelligence to expand market demand domestically and internationally, are a key determinant of firm performance. Nevertheless, future research is needed to understand further the choice of who become entrepreneurs and what are their characteristics in different settings. This research will require the use of matched employer-employee data as well as more qualitative evidence on firms and individuals in low- and middle-income countries. Better data on measures such as intangible capital, supplier-buyer networks, and organization are also needed to understand how firms accumulate capabilities.

Notes

1 | Jones (2013) discusses China and Singapore as typical examples of such impact, where multinational enterprises helped to create the leading exporting companies.

2 | For the rest of this chapter, we refer to firms or establishments synonymously as "firms."

3 | For example, the number of employees might be misreported due to informal employment, value added might be inflated by local authorities to meet targets, and revenues and expenses might be misreported for tax purposes (Holz 2014; Joshi, Hasan, and Amoranto 2009).

4 | For an influential argument along these lines, see Hsieh and Klenow 2014.

5 | See appendix G for details about the variables used in this analysis and their availability across countries.

6 | To have comparable age cohorts, we are limited by the short panel length in some countries. Further, the small number of firms that survive beyond five years in small economies makes extending cohort length unconducive for statistical analysis. To maximize sample size, we pool all available five-year cohorts in the data in each country, which results in one or multiple cohorts depending on the panel length. For example, Vietnam has only one cohort that entered and survived between 2007 and 2012. Other countries such as Serbia had as many as five cohorts that entered in each year from 2006 to 2011.

7 | Specifically, indicators of the firm-size group include the following:

- Firms that are large at entry (t_0) and large in year five (t_5)
- Firms that begin as small or medium in t_0 and grow large in t_5
- Other firms who survive in t_5 at small or medium size
- Nonsurviving firms in t_5 : exiting at t_1, t_2, t_3, and t_4 respectively.

8 | In the pooled results, they are also significantly smaller than other SMEs that did not survive or grow large. This result is driven by China and Indonesia, however.

9 | See appendix G for a discussion of the caveat regarding comparing capital and investment across countries.

10 | Caliendo and Rossi-Hansberg (2012), Caliendo, Monte, and Rossi-Hansberg (2015), and Cruz, Bussolo, and Iacovone (2018) find support for this argument, showing that an export promotion program in Brazil induced firms to reorganize by adding more layers, reduced average wages in all preexisting layers, and improved their export performance.

11 | In the case of Côte d'Ivoire, the layers include unskilled employees, technical and professional employees, managers, and executives. Average workers in a higher layer earn more, and the typical firm uses fewer of them.

References

Arkolakis, Costas. 2016. "A Unified Theory of Firm Selection and Growth." *Quarterly Journal of Economics* 131 (1): 89–155.

Azoulay, Pierre, Benjamin Jones, J. Daniel Kim, and Javier Miranda. 2018. "Age and High-Growth Entrepreneurship." Working Paper 18-11, Institute for Policy Research, Northwestern University, Evanston, IL.

Bastos, Paulo, Joana Silva, and Rafael Prado Proenca. 2018. "Exports and Job Training." Policy Research Working Paper 7676, World Bank, Washington, DC.

Bernard, Andrew B., Emmanuel Dhyne, Glenn Magerman, Kalina Manova, and Andreas Moxnes. 2019. "The Origins of Firm Heterogeneity: A Production Network Approach." NBER Working Paper 25441, National Bureau of Economic Research, Cambridge, MA.

Bloom, Nicholas, Gregory Fischer, Imran Rasul, Andres Rodriguez-Clare, Tavneet Suri, Christopher Udry, Eric Verhoogen, Christopher Woodruff, and Giulia Zane. 2014. "Firm Capabilities and Economic Growth." Evidence Paper, International Growth Centre, London.

Bruhn, Miriam, and Lisa Xu. 2019. *On the Origins of Large and Fast-Growing Firms around the World.* Washington, DC: World Bank.

Burkart, Mike, Fausto Panunzi, and Andrei Shleifer. 2003. "Family Firms." *Journal of Finance* 58 (5): 2167–201.

Cabral, Luís M. B., and José Mata. 2003. "On the Evolution of the Firm Size Distribution: Facts and Theory." *American Economic Review* 93 (4): 1075–90.

Caliendo, Lorenzo, Ferdinando Monte, and Esteban Rossi-Hansberg. 2015. "The Anatomy of French Production Hierarchies." *Journal of Political Economy* 123 (4) 809–52.

Caliendo, Lorenzo, and Esteban Rossi-Hansberg. 2012. "The Impact of Trade on Organization and Productivity." *Quarterly Journal of Economics* 127 (3): 1393–467.

Cruz, Marcio, Maurizio Bussolo, and Leonardo Iacovone. 2018. "Organizing Knowledge to Compete: Impacts of Capacity Building Programs on Firm Organization." *Journal of International Economics* 111 (March): 1–20.

Cusolito, Ana Paula, and William F. Maloney. 2018. *Productivity Revisited: Shifting Paradigms in Analysis and Policy.* Washington, DC: World Bank.

Eaton, Jonathan, Samuel Kortum, and Francis Kramarz. 2011. "An Anatomy of International Trade: Evidence from French Firms." *Econometrica* 79 (5): 1453–98.

Eeckhout, Jan, and Philipp Kircher. 2018. "Assortative Matching with Large Firms." *Econometrica* 86 (1): 85–132.

Foster, Lucia, John Haltiwanger, and Chad Syverson. 2016. "The Slow Growth of New Plants: Learning about Demand?" *Economica* 83 (329): 91–129.

Freund, Caroline. 2016. *Rich People Poor Countries: The Rise of Emerging-Market Tycoons and Their Mega Firms.* Washington, DC: Peterson Institute for International Economics.

Freund, Caroline, and Martha Denisse Pierola. 2015. "Export Superstars." *Review of Economics and Statistics* 97 (5): 1023–32.

Freund, Caroline, and Martha Denisse Pierola. 2016. "The Origins and Dynamics of Export Superstars." Working Paper 16-11, Peterson Institute for International Economics, Washington, DC.

Goswami, Arti Grover, Denis Medvedev, and Ellen Olafsen. 2019. *High-Growth Firms: Facts, Fiction, and Policy Options for Emerging Economies.* Washington, DC: World Bank.

Gupta, Vishal K., Seonghee Han, Sandra C. Mortal, Sabatino Silveri, and Daniel B. Turban. 2018. "Do Women CEOs Face Greater Threat of Shareholder Activism Compared to Male CEOs? A Role Congruity Perspective." *Journal of Applied Psychology* 103 (2): 228–36.

Haskel, Jonathan, and Stian Westlake. 2017. *Capitalism without Capital: The Rise of the Intangible Economy.* Princeton, NJ: Princeton University Press.

Hoffmann Erik P., and Frederic J. Fleron Jr., eds. 1980. *The Conduct of Soviet Foreign Policy.* New York: Aldine.

Holz, Carsten A. 2014. "The Quality of China's GDP Statistics." *China Economic Review* 30 (September): 309–38.

Hopenhayn, Hugo A. 1992. "Entry, Exit, and Firm Dynamics in Long-Run Equilibrium." *Econometrica* 60 (5): 1127–50.

Hottman, Colin J., Stephen J. Redding, and David E. Weinstein. 2016. "Quantifying the Sources of Firm Heterogeneity." *Quarterly Journal of Economics* 131 (3): 1291–364.

Hsieh, Chang-Tai, and Peter J. Klenow. 2014. "The Life Cycle of Plants in India and Mexico." *Quarterly Journal of Economics* 129 (3): 1035–84.

Jones, Geoffrey. 2013. *Entrepreneurship and Multinationals: Global Business and the Making of the Modern World.* Cheltenham, UK: Edward Elgar.

Joshi, Kaushal, Rana Hasan, and Glenita Amoranto. 2009. "Surveys of Informal Sector Enterprises—Some Measurement Issues." ADB Economics Working Paper 183, Asia Development Bank, Manila.

Jovanovic, Boyan. 1989. "Selection and the Evolution of Industry." *Econometrica* 50 (3): 649–70.

Klepper, Steven, and Sally Sleeper. 2005. "Entry by Spinoffs." *Management Science* 51 (8): 1291–306.

Lafontaine, Francine, and Kathryn Shaw. 2014. "Serial Entrepreneurship: Learning by Doing?" NBER Working Paper 20312, National Bureau of Economic Research, Cambridge, MA.

Lemos, Renata, and Daniela Scur. 2018. "All in the Family? CEO Choice and Firm Organization." CEP Discussion Paper 1528, Centre for Economic Performance, London School of Business, London.

Luttmer, Erzo G. J. 2011. "On the Mechanics of Firm Growth." *Review of Economic Studies* 78 (3): 1042–68.

Melitz, Marc J. 2003. "The Impact of Trade on Intra-Industry Reallocations and Aggregate Industry Productivity." *Econometrica* 71 (6): 1695–725.

Merotto, Dino, Michael Weber, and Reyes Aterido. 2018. "Pathways to Better Jobs in IDA Countries: Findings from Jobs Diagnostics." Job Series 14, World Bank, Washington, DC.

Muendler, Marc-Andreas, and James E. Rauch. 2018. "Do Employee Spinoffs Learn Markets from Their Parents? Evidence from International Trade." NBER Working Paper 24302, National Bureau of Economic Research, Cambridge, MA.

OECD (Organisation for Economic Co-operation and Development). Various years. DynEmp (Measuring Job Creation by Start-ups and Young Firms) database. Paris: OECD, Directorate for Science, Technology and Innovation. http://www.oecd.org.sti.dynemp.htm.

OECD (Organisation for Economic Co-operation and Development). Various years. Orbis database. Paris: OECD.

Prescott, Edward C., and Michael Visscher. 1980. "Organization Capital." *Journal of Political Economy* 88 (3): 446–61.

Pugsley, Benjamin, Petr Sedlacek, and Vincent Sterk. 2018. "The Nature of Firm Growth." CEPR Discussion Paper 12670, Centre for Economic Policy Research, London.

Rijkers, Bob, Caroline Freund, and Antonio Nucifora. 2017. "All in the Family: State Capture in Tunisia." *Journal of Development Economics* 124 (C): 41–59.

Roberts, Mark J., Daniel Yi Xu, Xiaoyan Fan, and Shengxing Zhang. 2018. "The Role of Firm Factors in Demand, Cost, and Export Market Selection for Chinese Footwear Producers." *Review of Economic Studies* 85 (4): 2429–61.

Sabel, Charles, Eduardo Fernández-Arias, Ricardo Hausmann, Andrés Rodríguez-Clare, and Ernesto Stein, eds. 2012. *Export Pioneers in Latin America*. Washington, DC: David Rockefeller Center for Latin America Studies and Inter-American Development Bank.

Schoar, Antoinette. 2010. "The Divide between Subsistence and Transformational Entrepreneurship." In *Innovation Policy and the Economy*, vol. 10, edited by Josh Lerner and Scott Stern, 57–81. Chicago: University of Chicago Press.

Sutton, John. 2014. *An Enterprise Map of Mozambique*. London: International Growth Centre.

Sutton, John, and Nebil Kellow. 2010. *An Enterprise Map of Ethiopia*. London: International Growth Centre.

Sutton John, and Bennett Kpentey. 2012. *An Enterprise Map of Ghana*. London: International Growth Centre.

Sutton, John, and Gilian Langmead. 2013. *An Enterprise Map of Zambia*. London: International Growth Centre.

Sutton, John, and Donath Olomi. 2012. *An Enterprise Map of Tanzania*. London: International Growth Centre.

Van Biesebroeck, Johannes. 2005. "Firm Size Matters: Growth and Productivity Growth in African Manufacturing." *Economic Development and Cultural Change* 53 (3): 548–83.

World Bank. 2019. *World Development Report 2019: The Changing Nature of Work*. Washington, DC: World Bank.

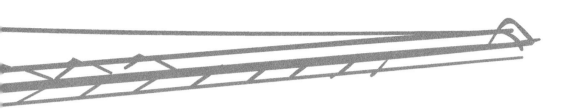

4. Supporting large-firm creation

Scale of production and productivity translate into better outcomes for firms and markets. But scale does not reach its full potential in low- and middle-income countries: the evidence points to a large-firm deficiency, both in the number of large firms and in the development benefits they generate. The shortage is most acute in the larger of large firms and the more efficient ones. These firms are often born different from the rest: they often start off large, build on existing skills and capital, organize production differently, and pursue strategies for market access that distinguish them from the rest from day one. Small and medium enterprise (SME) development is therefore important but unlikely to fill the gap on its own.

In light of this evidence, this concluding chapter explores a more balanced approach to supporting firm creation and growth that facilitates the emergence of large and productive firms, while still ensuring that their market power does not become entrenched and other firms have the space they need to thrive. We argue that policies to support SMEs should remain important within the agendas of low- and middle-income countries, but they should be complemented with policies to support large-firm creation from other sources through broad-based competition spurring foreign direct investment and spinoffs of other large firms.

Governments have an important role to play in fostering large-firm creation, through the correction of market failures that prevent the main ingredients of firm growth from coming into play—market access, technology, capital, labor, and managerial talent—rather than through the creation of state-owned ventures. Attention to the sources of large-firm creation—domestic mobilization, foreign investment, and entrepreneurship—combined with an effort to make markets contestable and operationally friendly to scale would go a long way toward filling the large-firm gap.

In much of the low- and middle-income world, these priorities are often less complex than they seem. For low-income countries, where many sources of large-firm creation are weak, medium- to long-term efforts should focus on improving institutions, competition authorities and frameworks, infrastructure, access to finance, and foreign investment. In the future, technological change stands to erode some of the key contributions of large firms to development, while increasing these firms' market reach and their impact on other dimensions. Keeping market contestability as the guiding principle for large-firm creation will enable markets to adapt and work for the largest possible number of participants.

What types of constraints give rise to the "missing top"?

Barriers to large-firm creation are numerous at time of birth yet go well beyond entry. Investors internalize a stream of future revenues and costs in their decision to enter a market, making a wide array of frictions to operation relevant for their decision. In what follows, we highlight an illustrative set of barriers, both at entry and beyond.

Market contestability

Perfectly contestable markets, as defined by Baumol's seminal 1982 work, are those with zero entry and exit costs—that is, no barriers, such as sunk costs and contractual agreements—and readily available industrial technology. In essence, they are markets where any new supplier could challenge incumbents on equal terms, undercutting their ability to extract rents and sustain inefficiencies.

Perfectly contestable markets do not exist in the real world: some markets are more contestable than others. But using contestability as a guide can foster large-firm creation and grow its beneficiaries without recourse to state ownership or highly restrictive business regulation, which have been used extensively in the past to these ends. Market contestability benefits, in principle, entrants of all sizes. In practice, however, restrictions in many sectors of economic activity are of higher relevance to large entrants or firms that grow to scale. Regulatory restrictions, such as statutory monopolies and oligopolies, preferential access to natural resources and government contracts, or barriers to foreign competitors, are often designed to prevent entry at scale. Increasing market contestability ultimately facilitates entry at scale or growth to scale, which can challenge incumbents, improve efficiency, and increase the benefits to consumers. Entry costs and barriers as well as the availability of relevant know-how to compete are in many ways dependent on the nature of economic activity. But governments have a role in improving contestability. Regulatory protection of incumbents, closed markets through licensing, or barriers to trade and investment all fall within the scope of what governments can address to that end.

Low- and middle-income countries have important ground to cover. First, many of these countries offer significantly greater protection to incumbents than higher-income economies. Over the period 2013–16, lower-middle-income countries exhibited protection levels about 20 percent higher than levels in upper-middle-income countries and about 70 percent higher than levels in high-income countries (figure 4.1). Such institutional barriers prevent the emergence of new large firms that could contest the market. The differential protection from import competition further distorts the allocation of resources toward less-competitive firms.

International trade and the establishment of foreign firms can be a source of strong pressure that increases market contestability. Because free trade increases the extent of the market, it also raises the viable number of participants. Trade,

FIGURE 4.1 Levels of protection of large incumbent firms across countries at different income levels

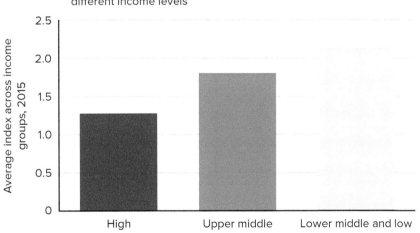

Source: Calculations based on Organisation for Economic Co-operation and Development (OECD) and World Bank indicators of product market regulation and competition data (Koske et al. 2015).

therefore, is a sine qua non for firm growth in countries that are otherwise too small or too poor to support production at scale. Their comparative advantages remain untapped without exposure to global demand. Moreover, for exporters and investors establishing affiliates abroad, technological barriers to entry and the associated sunk costs have already been incurred elsewhere, bringing about a potent pool of potential challengers to incumbents in markets where they enter.

But reducing entry barriers is not sufficient to generate contestable markets. Left unregulated, large businesses will have an incentive to deter subsequent entry, a situation that calls for public intervention through legislation, surveillance, and enforcement of competition policy. The case of South Africa is illustrative in that respect: inefficient state ownership can be replaced by inefficient private or foreign ownership of large firms that pursue uncompetitive practices and contribute little to development (box 4.1).

BOX 4.1   Privatization and foreign ownership do not guarantee contestable markets: The case of South Africa's steel industry

The South African economy is characterized by high barriers to entry and high levels of concentration. Large firms play an important role; however, they also perpetuate some of the challenges in the structure of the economy. Many of the dominant firms in the economy have links to South Africa's colonial history through the privatization of state-owned enterprises.

The South African Iron and Steel Industrial Corporation Limited (Iscor) was founded in 1928 as a statutory parastatal. Iscor was privatized in 1989, and its shares were listed on the Johannesburg Stock Exchange. In the mid-1990s (after the apartheid era), it became apparent that structural transformation was required through beneficiation—additional processing that improves the economic value of the ores. In 2001 Iscor's steel and mining operations were divided into two separately listed companies: Kumba Resources (iron ore mining) and Iscor (steel production). Iscor is now owned by ArcelorMittal South Africa (AMSA), a multinational group that holds 68 percent of shares.

The lack of competition persisted after privatization and foreign takeover. For 25 years, AMSA benefited immensely from cheap energy cost agreements from the 1990s and the guaranteed iron ore supply at cost plus a

3 percent management fee, which were set in place when Iscor's steel and mining operations were unbundled. Its main competitor, Evraz Highveld Steel, closed down its operations in February 2016 due to the downturn in commodity prices and competition from subsidized steel imports from China.

AMSA's dominant position in the market has allowed the company to undertake anticompetitive behavior in the South African economy. In 2008 the Competition Commission initiated an investigation against long and flat steel producers in South Africa following concerns about high and rising prices of steel products, despite South Africa being a net exporter of steel. AMSA was involved in two cartels and flat steel price fixing. AMSA admitted to taking part in these cartels and price fixing and agreed to pay a R1.5 billion administrative penalty. Evraz was also fined R1 million for its involvement in flat steel price fixing.

Despite restructuring, upstream industries have continued to dominate the domestic steel industry, making the steel industry a good example of how ownership transition and foreign investment do not by themselves lead to more competitive markets.

Source: National Treasury of South Africa.

What does this public intervention consist of in practice? Competition law and policy require an independent, competent authority with the means to survey the market for evidence of price-fixing agreements or abuse of dominance, discrimination, or predatory pricing and the power to penalize and thereby deter anticompetitive conduct. These authorities, the mandates to survey, or the capacity to deliver are often absent in lower-income countries (World Bank 2016). Beyond competition law, economic regulation is meant to simulate competition to encourage or induce firms to operate efficiently in sectors where market failures are widespread. Pricing rules, such as the adoption of upper and lower bounds for the prices of firms considered to possess market power, can replicate the bounds that market pressures would enforce under perfect contestability in the case of natural oligopolies (Baumol 1982). Often, several regulatory options exist to address valid public policy objectives—such as labor, social, or environmental protection—which are all associated with better development outcomes. Governments should choose regulatory options that are the least restrictive to competition (for example, setting and enforcing standards rather than outright banning additional operators of certain activities).

Perceptions of the intensity of competition and effectiveness of government policies across countries and income groups are revealing of the ground that low- and middle-income countries have to cover in these areas. The lower the income, the lower the scores on both indicators over the last decade (figure 4.2). The fact that governments are relatively ineffective at enforcing competition resonates with the evidence that the scope for informal or formal anticompetitive arrangements is greater in these markets (Hallward-Driemeier and Pritchett 2015).

Trends point to a reason for further action: while significant improvements were recorded in the first part of the decade, perceptions of competitive

FIGURE 4.2 Opposite trends in perceptions of competition and effectiveness of government policies across income groups, 2007–17

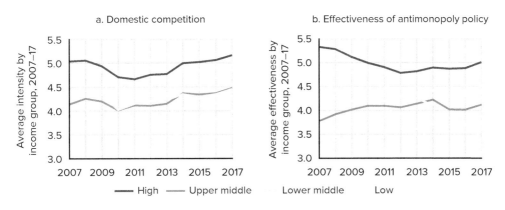

Source: Schwab 2019. Calculations based on the World Economic Forum Global Investment Competitiveness data (2019).

pressure remained largely unchanged since 2014, and the effectiveness of policies has weakened. In higher-income countries, executives perceive an intensification of competition, possibly due to increasing concentration of market power among a handful of frontier firms (Andrews, Criscuolo, and Gal 2016), with which the majority of firms find it harder to compete. The trend is not followed in low- and middle-income countries.

Ultimately, low contestability stands to affect both firm performance and large-firm entry. Not only will large firms in noncontestable markets fall short on delivering the same development benefits; their protected status will prevent other large firms that can provide such benefits from entering the market.

Business environment constraints are internalized in the decision to enter

Even in theoretically perfectly contestable markets, entrants need to have an operational advantage over incumbents to be able to grow (see Stiglitz's critique of Baumol's theory contestability; Stiglitz 1987). Firms internalize these operational advantages and constraints in the decision to enter a market, which are neither size-neutral nor the same across countries at different income levels.

In low- and middle-income countries, cross-country empirical studies document a range of regulations that can disincentivize the growth of firms beyond smallness. Large firms often bear the brunt of business regulation. Corporate tax systems, for example, often focus enforcement efforts on larger firms, where they can maximize potential revenues at minimum cost. As a result, the effective tax rates for smaller firms may be lower, creating incentives for firms to stay small. As discussed in the introduction, other regulatory taxes—such as wage regulations, hiring and firing restrictions, social security contributions, and reporting requirements—are often applied at specific employment thresholds, creating incentives to remain small.

The large-firm "tax" is highest in low-income countries. The World Bank Enterprise Surveys, compiled for 123 countries over the 2006–18 period, allow analysis of constraints facing firms in different areas—from regulation to competition and infrastructure—that other surveys cannot support across countries and industries. The likelihood that large firms will report a certain factor as constraining gives some inkling of its *severity*, while the difference between that likelihood across firms of different sizes tells us more about the *specificity* of this constraint on large-firm operations (see box 4.2 for details of the estimation). Several findings in that respect are worth noting.

First, the extent to which areas of the business environment are viewed as constraints tends to decrease with national income, not only for SMEs but also for large firms. In general, constraints on operations are viewed as more severe in low-income countries, but the degree to which those constraints affect large firms specifically is also higher (figure 4.3). For instance,

BOX 4.2   Severity and specificity analysis for constraints reported in World Bank
Enterprise Surveys

The analysis on constraints by firm size made use of World Bank Enterprise Survey data, a firm-level survey of a representative sample of an economy's private sector. The surveys cover a broad range of business environment topics, including access to finance, corruption, infrastructure, crime, competition, and performance measures. Enterprise Surveys from 123 countries were drawn on, using the latest survey years available (all between 2006 and 2018).

Using a linear probability model, the severity of any business constraint was modeled with the following specification:

$$y_{isc} = \beta_0 + \beta_L Large + D_c + D_s + \varepsilon_{isc},$$

where the dependent variable, y_{isc}, is a binary variable that is equal to 1 if the firm indicates that the obstacle in question is a moderate, major, or very severe obstacle to its operations. *Large* is a binary variable indicating whether a firm has more than 100 employees; D_c and D_s are country and sector fixed effects. This regression was run separately for each obstacle across three groups of countries (low-income, lower-middle-income, and upper-middle-income countries).

Through this regression, we report $(\beta_0 + \beta_L)$ as the probability that a constraint is severe for large firms in a country group, while β_L as the probability that a constraint is *specific* to large firms in a country group.

FIGURE 4.3   Large firms face more severe constraints on operations in low-income countries

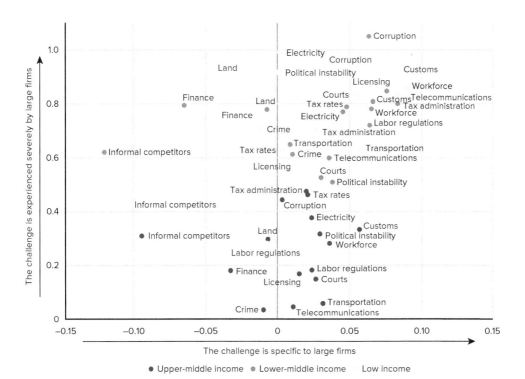

Source: Calculations based on World Bank Enterprise Survey data (2018).
Note: Severity and specificity of challenges for large firms are calculated according to the methodology outlined in box 4.2 for countries in different income groups.

the average probability that any factor will be viewed as a constraint on operations is 26 percent in upper-middle-income countries, compared with about 74 percent in low-income countries. The additional probability that the factor will be viewed as constraining business for large firms is only 1 percent in upper-middle-income countries, compared with 3 percent in low-income countries. This suggests that constraints on operations in low-income countries will particularly affect the operations of large establishments, reducing large-firm density.

Second, large firms and SMEs face different types of constraints on their operations. Large establishments often have particular advantages that make them more resilient to certain aspects of the policy environment and conditions. At the global level, evidence suggests that they are less likely than SMEs to be affected by credit constraints and less likely to be affected by competition from firms operating in the informal sector (figure 4.3). Issues like crime and access to land are also less severe deterrents for large-firm operations. As a more general finding, government-led functions and institutions—such as courts, customs, regulations, and infrastructure—have both a high severity and a disproportionate impact on large-firm operations. This is especially true in low-income countries, a finding that is not surprising, as smaller firms in these contexts can more easily fall under the government's radar and pursue operations with only partial compliance to relevant regulation.

Large firms are also affected disproportionately by workforce issues, corroborating the results from previous chapters, which detail important differences between firms that grow large and those that stay small or medium, in terms of the physical, managerial, and human capital. Both large firms that start off large and SMEs that grow large are often skill-intensive companies that build on prior experience strongly suited to the business, either in the same sector, in other large enterprises, or in finance. Large firms also hire more experienced and generally higher-skill workers with industry-specific expertise.

A corollary to the differential impacts of regulation on large firms and SMEs is that, even when regulations are applied uniformly across the firm-size distribution, the impact may be greater for larger enterprises. In other words, uniformly applied policies do not constrain firms uniformly. For example, large firms disproportionately bear the burden of cumbersome or complex customs operations because they tend to export more, even if objective data suggest that SMEs face the same average costs, wait times, and the like. Recent research suggests, also, that large firms differentially benefit from big data technology because, with a higher volume of economic activity and a longer firm history, they have more data to process. Fully understanding the constraints on entry and operations of large firms depends on understanding the factors that are important for large-firm operations.

How to foster large-firm creation?

Little empirical analysis has been devoted to understanding the policies and actions that contribute to changes in the size distribution of firms. As a result, it is difficult to draw general lessons from the strategies that individual countries have pursued to increase the presence of large firms.

Four main sources of large-firm creation are identified in chapter 3: domestic investment mobilization, foreign direct investment (FDI), government sponsorship, and entrepreneurship (start-up firms that grow to scale). In the absence of private sources of large firms, governments have often resorted to state-owned firms to create markets, boost export competitiveness, and spur the benefits of commerce to societies. The vast majority of these experiences have failed to deliver, and state-owned ventures still represent large contingent liabilities for governments around the world. Governments today have an important role to play in fostering large-firm creation by correcting market failures that prevent production from reaching scale play—market access, technology, capital, labor, and managerial talent—rather than by running state-owned ventures. Various strategies, which are often complementary, exist to encourage the growth of large firms, to which we now turn.

Industrial policies and domestic investment mobilization

Industrial policy in large part coincides with facilitating large-firm development by mobilizing domestic investment. Large firms often benefit heavily from industrial policies, whether aimed at supporting scale per se or supporting the buildup of specific sectors and activities. Many of these policies and experiences have grown from country efforts to rebalance economic growth toward manufacturing with the aim of reaping productivity improvements and entry into global value chains. A central feature of large firms—economies of scale and scope—are particularly important in manufacturing.

The Republic of Korea's industrial development exemplifies this perspective, as it went hand in hand with the promotion of large industry. Over several decades, Korea saw a significant rise in employment in technology-driven large industrial firms, steered by a systematic identification of the human and technological constraints on fast growth combined with intense support for family-owned industrial conglomerates (chaebols). The chaebols played an important role in developing Korea's export capabilities into new products and markets and were instrumental in Korea's growth. Their growth was heavily aided by direct government support in the form of contracts, legislative support, tax benefits, foreign exchange allocations, and cheap credit. Pursuing a policy of guided or managed capitalism and taking advantage of its control of the banking system, the government granted easy and cheap access to capital as well as control over imports that could compete with the chaebols, ensuring their ability to dominate the market (Doral and Patrono 2010). In return, the chaebols agreed to make large investments in export-oriented industries. The government even guaranteed repayment should a company be unable to repay its foreign creditors.[1]

In Korea, support for large firms was coupled with value chain development and support for smaller firms. At the beginning, the focus of industrial policies was on promoting industries with scale economies by means of exports. In the country's third and fourth five-year development plans in the 1970s, SMEs received strong support to supply parts and components to heavy and chemical industries. This balance was very effective: SMEs bloomed due to local content initiatives.

But direct support for large firms also contributed to entrenched market power. As large-firm productivity has the potential to raise the barriers to entry for new (and potentially smaller) competitors, large-firm positions can become entrenched, allowing them to exploit their market power.[2] This situation may be particularly acute in low- and middle-income countries, lacking competitive markets. The rise of the chaebols was instrumental in transforming Korea's economy, but as their size and influence grew, they became increasingly difficult to control (Naval Post-Graduate School 2014). A major driver of resilience for the chaebols' productivity is that they are exposed to international competition.

Special support for large firms can also be inefficient. Industrial policies and support geared toward larger firms may result in financial outlays without positively affecting large-firm behavior. Industrial policies in the United Kingdom designed to raise productivity and employment across firms of all sizes have been found to have no treatment effect on larger firms, with impacts limited to smaller firms (Criscuolo et al. 2012). Large firms could be more able to game the system and benefit from program incentives without changing investment or employment decisions. Ultimately, concerns about governments' ability to "pick winners" and identify distortions, which are highly dependent on market structure and the nature of economic activity as well as corruption around the process, often introduce further distortions than the ones industrial policies are designed to remedy (Freund 2016).

There has been no consensus to date over the exact ingredients of success for industrial policies. In the last decade, there has been renewed emphasis on these strategies in both high-income and low- and middle-income countries to address new needs for integrating and upgrading global value chains as well as developing the knowledge economy (United Nations 2019). A recent global stocktaking by the United Nations highlighted three main directions that capture about one-third of more than 110 industrial policy schemes around the world: horizontal facilitation policies with measures to promote the buildup of specific industrial sectors—focusing mostly on (a) natural-resource-based (processing) industries and light manufacturing, (b) horizontal policies having industry-specific *catch-up* objectives in higher-skill manufacturing industries (engineering industries), and (c) mostly in high-income countries, specific focus on the development of advanced manufacturing, driven by the New Industrial Revolution. These new policies are increasingly designed to include or connect small and medium enterprises, preserve market contestability, and integrate with other policy areas to respond to broader issues such as sustainable development. The current thinking is summarized well by three key principles that are widely thought to underpin the success of the Asian industrial policies of the last decades (Cherif and Hasanov 2019): (a) state intervention to fix market failures; (b) export orientation, in contrast to import substitution; and (c) the pursuit of fierce competition both abroad and domestically, with strict accountability.

Foreign direct investment

Multinational enterprises have advantages in terms of productivity, scale, and market access that challenge incumbents in ways that no other entrant can. They typically enter at a scale that is larger than domestic start-ups and with prospects for growth that are significantly more positive (World Bank 2020). At the same time, they face barriers due to their foreignness against which they typically evaluate returns from entry into a new market.

Because of their value addition—jobs, tax revenue, and aggregate productivity—almost all economies have policies and investment strategies aimed in part at recruiting large multinational enterprises to operate in their country. These strategies can result in significant increases in the share of large firms in a short period of time. With FDI declining worldwide—from 5.3 percent of gross domestic product (GDP) in 2007 to 2.3 percent in 2017 (figure 4.4)—low-income countries must compete for ever scarcer investments, suggesting a potentially declining source of large-firm creation in these contexts.

A large empirical literature provides insights on the factors that have proved important for countries to attract FDI inflows—both policy-related and non-policy factors. Along with the market size of the host country, its remoteness, factor endowments, and political and economic stability, factors on the policy side include discriminatory regulation as well as typical constraints that large domestic firms face, such as regulation imposing additional labor costs, market arrangements, corporate tax rates, infrastructure, trade barriers, and product-market regulation (World Bank 2018b).

The constraints on FDI differ from country to country, and so do the reform agendas. The United Nations' latest data on related policy trends across the world show that, in the last year alone, one-third of new policy measures

FIGURE 4.4   Low-income countries must compete for ever-scarcer foreign direct investment

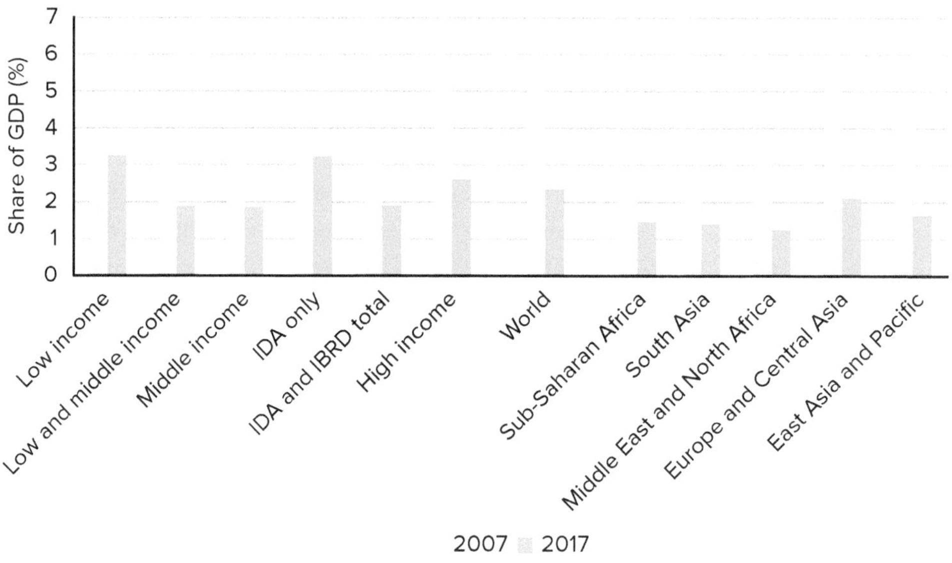

2007 ▢ 2017

Source: Calculations based on World Development Indicators data (2019).
Note: IBRD = International Bank for Reconstruction and Development. IDA = International Development Association.

toward FDI restricted or regulated investment more tightly, while two-thirds of new measures liberalized and promoted FDI (United Nations 2019). This is the highest share of restrictive and regulatory measures over the last 15 years, although the world as a whole has become more liberal toward investment.

Sub-Saharan Africa attracts the lowest level of FDI as a share of GDP worldwide, but some countries have made giant advances in creating an enabling framework for FDI, and they have seen strong results. One of them is Sierra Leone, whose government has actively encouraged private investment over the last decade by establishing a one-stop shop for investors, the Sierra Leone Investment and Export Promotion Agency; implementing key trade promotion activities under the Integrated Framework; and as revising legal and regulatory frameworks. The country offers an open and friendly FDI regulatory regime and firm guarantees against expropriation (investor protection), and most business sectors are fully open to foreign equity ownership (the Investment Promotion Act offers a level playing field for all domestic and foreign investors with respect to ownership of local companies) (Siddiqi 2016). Since 2007, the share of inward FDI has increased from 4.4 percent of GDP to 14.8 percent.

During the 2007–17 period, Ethiopia dramatically improved its share of FDI (with FDI as a share of GDP increasing from 1.1 percent to 5.0 percent) through the privatization of huge state-owned companies, institutional reform, and construction of industrial parks in special economic zones. Because the reforms and investments needed to attract foreign investment can be extensive and difficult to achieve, low-income countries have looked to special economic zones as a way to ring-fence market-oriented reforms and build experience that can then be implemented more widely.

Ultimately, FDI is one route to grow a large-firm presence in low-income economies, but the extent to which the domestic economy benefits from multinational ventures varies. While there is clear evidence that FDI can have a positive impact on the domestic productivity of host countries, certain "mediating factors" are needed, such as the productivity of foreign investors, the absorptive capacity of host firms, and the institutional frameworks of the host economy. Large firms benefit the domestic economy by crowding in other investment and technology transfers and the transmission of new managerial ideas and skills. Any factors that inhibit this crowding in of domestic and labor markets, as well as foreign markets, will naturally result in lower benefits from FDI (Munemo 2015).

By their nature, the domestic links of foreign multinational companies tend, on average, to be less strong than those of domestic firms, with very few exceptions (Lejárraga and Ragoussis 2018). Part of this variation could be due to industrial activities where multinational firms are concentrated. Yet in countries with large markets—such as China, India, Indonesia, and Nigeria—both multinationals and domestic firms exhibit strong local sourcing. This is due to the availability of local inputs for a variety of activities and also to the intensity of market-seeking FDI in addition to other types of investments. Large firms created through FDI therefore stand to benefit the local economies, though to a varying extent that depends primarily on the context.

Supporting entrepreneurship and SME growth

With few large firms to begin with, low- and middle-income countries need to support start-ups of new firms, even though high failure rates mean that few of them will grow to become large firms. Almost all low- and middle-income countries have policies to promote SMEs. They range from incubation platforms to small business financial support to tax incentives. Increasingly, policy makers recognize that, while the SME segment as a whole can benefit from better access to finance, capacity building, and more, only a small proportion of SMEs have the potential to become large firms. Hence, many governments also pursue more targeted policies toward "small and growing businesses," or "gazelles," that have the potential to grow into large firms.

The challenge for government policy in the area of entrepreneurship has become how to transform the competitive basis of SMEs from one of exploiting labor to one of exploiting technology. Measures to support high-growth SMEs must include ways for small business to tap the knowledge of experienced entrepreneurs. A platform of knowledge and access to information is crucial for picking business opportunities and for creating better-functioning, robust networks and linkages between entrepreneurs.

The model used by Taiwan, China, has been successful in this respect. The economy adopted the "second mover" strategy of entering the global high-tech market only after products matured by working on the capability of domestic firms to deliver them (Amsden and Chu 2003). Government-funded research institutes were important in implementing the strategy. They assimilated advanced technology from abroad, then diffused the technology to smaller, local firms. The institutes have also increasingly served as the platform for coordinating the development of indigenous technology. As a result, many firms that started as SMEs in Taiwan, China, have enhanced their technological and innovative capabilities and have upgraded in their global value chains. These innovation financing policies, together with the intermediary role of government research institutes, have been major drivers of that transition. During the 1990s, the schemes began to focus more on helping firms to develop new products, enhancing research and development capabilities, and encouraging the emergence of start-up companies in new sectors such as biotechnology.

Technology changes large-firm creation, growth, and impact

The emergence of new technologies of production, such as automation, and new technologies of distribution, such as digital platforms, have many implications for the ways in which firms enter and grow to scale. Three main effects can be identified. First, new technologies allow firms to increase their market reach, which boosts the returns of entrants with incremental innovation, even in markets that are remote or small. While many of these technologies are widely available to new entrants, they require skills and complementary services to deliver their benefits (De Stefano, Kneller, and Timmis 2018), which entrants in low-income countries may have difficulty obtaining. Even if, in principle, these technologies allow smaller entrants to contest incumbents using information, price competition, and customization—the materialization of their benefits will depend on the development of a base of critical skills and complementary infrastructure. In low-income countries, it is argued that greater diffusion of existing rather than new technologies has the potential to bring substantial benefits to firms (Comin and Mestieri 2018).

Second, new frontier technologies of production—from artificial intelligence to biotechnology, energy, and transport—are being developed by an increasingly smaller number of lead firms in high-income and major emerging economies. These technologies allow firms to amass market power quickly and effectively deter the entry of other firms at global scale. Megafirms of that tier can challenge incumbents in lower-income economies effectively through FDI, but themselves would be increasingly difficult to challenge once they enter, leading to likely abuse of dominance. Lower-income countries might be ill prepared to address the resulting failures.

Third, new technologies stand to erode in some ways the value the addition of large firms in development terms, while increasing it in others. The automation of production and provision of digital services, for example, allow businesses to use less labor-intensive production and reduce demand for local intermediate goods and services, both of which are among the key developmental benefits of large firms. However, by growing their reach and revenue, these technologies can also generate greater tax revenue from the resulting economic activity.

One can argue that lower-income economies stand to benefit more from this balance of pros and cons because they remain focused on traditional low-technology and services sectors where market access remains the most important obstacle to entry and growth. With the right regulatory framework, access to existing technology in these markets can change large-firm creation and growth in ways that likely bring more benefits than costs. As countries upgrade with more sophisticated production, then safety nets, skills strategies, and industrial strategies become more important to balance the benefits that technology promises through scale, with all of its disadvantages.

What are the options for low-income countries?

While there are no generic formulas to achieving greater scale of production, there are some considerations that could be helpful to countries where sources of large-firm creation are weak. First, the evidence highlights that government-led functions and institutions have a disproportionate impact on large-firm operations and, by extension, large-firm creation in these countries. Improving the functioning of these institutions with better regulatory environments, trade facilitation, protection of property rights, and efficient tax regimes stands to make a difference for large firms, even when these long-term reforms do not have large-firm creation as the objective.

Where institutional enforcement capacity is limited, governments need to do all they can to make conditions as favorable as possible for pro-competitive behavior, which includes sustaining open trading regimes and avoiding the creation of obstacles to market contestability through poorly designed regulation or the granting of privileges to state-owned enterprises. This is the essence of the so-called "broad-based competition policy" defined to encompass all actions that governments may take to promote competition, including trade liberalization, measures to facilitate domestic and foreign entry into industry and services, the demonopolization of sectors, and imposition of hard budget constraints on public enterprises (Hoeckman and Holmes 1999).

In Africa, the policy reorientation required is often more basic than in countries at higher levels of development. Markets are often effectively closed, marked by a range of policies, procedures, and commercial decisions that reinforce noncontestability by restricting the number of firms or limiting investment in specific industries. Competition law is nascent, largely limited to the law defined under common markets, such as the Common Market for Eastern and Southern Africa, and focused primarily on cross-country mergers. Few countries have an applicable legislative regime in force to govern domestic conduct from an antitrust perspective (World Bank 2016). While competition law is becoming more active, only 32 countries (out of 54) had competition laws by 2015;[3] where laws exist, they are often not enforced because of weaknesses in regulatory bodies. Prioritization needs to be given to removing the most harmful anticompetitive practices and, in some cases, revising fines for companies practicing techniques designed to deter the entry of a prospective entrant (World Bank 2016).

Fostering productive and competitive large firms also requires the institutional capacity to deliver the changes needed for large-firm entry, innovation, and access to technology. The importance of a few large firms in driving growth stems from their critical role in the allocation of capital and labor for a country's potential output (Freund 2016). To unleash their potential, governments need to shift attention away from particular sectors and toward productive firms within every sector.

There are different ways of doing so. As noted in a recent World Bank report on productivity (Cirera and Maloney 2017), countries need to build institutional capacities to match specific policy goals for entrepreneurship. Low- and middle-income countries are often marked by enabling environments that do little to promote firm upgrading, which would allow them to realize catch-up gains, building on the ideas, products, and technologies of higher-income countries. With scarce government capacity, helping large firms to enact such upgrades would require policies to be sequenced in accordance with the capabilities of the private sector: a "capabilities escalator," which ratchets through progressively higher stages of sophistication.

Governments can also contribute significantly to the success of large firms by reducing informational barriers that hinder the adoption of good managerial and production processes and spreading digital technology that will allow them to access new markets. A huge variation is observed across establishments in the adoption of practices known to improve productivity and profitability, including quality control procedures, inventory management, and some human resources management practices. Making knowledge about good practices more broadly available can help small and potentially large companies to improve their productivity and expand their operations. Indeed, a recent study in India found that making free consulting services on management practices available to large textile firms led to a 17 percent increase in firm productivity during the first year and the opening of more production plants within three years (Bloom et al. 2013).

CASE STUDY
Large-firm creation in Guinea: Past, present, and future

Despite the fact that its economy has more than doubled in size in the past decade, Guinea remains one of the world's least-developed countries, with GDP per capita of US$827 (in 2017), well below the regional average of US$1,573. The Guinean private sector is composed largely of informal, small, rural, and low-revenue enterprises; 92 percent of Guinean businesses employ fewer than five people and generate annual revenue of less than US$7,000 (APIP 2016). Despite the challenging context, the government has options to foster the creation and growth of large firms.

The landscape of firms

Formal Guinean firms operate in a limited set of sectors and are dominated by a small group of business elites (World Bank 2019). Very few are large in size, mainly in extractives, agriculture, and, recently, energy. Manufacturing is confined to 100 or so formal enterprises, producing mainly flour, beer, fruit juice, mineral water, edible oils, cement, cotton, soap, and chemical products (World Bank 2019). Most of these enterprises enjoy a monopoly or virtual monopoly in domestic goods but face strong competition from imported products (WTO 2018). Few enterprises export, as reflected in the small number of products approved under the Economic Community of West African States, free-trade regime. In the agribusiness sector, and despite favorable agroclimatic conditions, governance and institutional challenges have resulted in massive underperformance and missed opportunities. Formal private sector activity is limited, especially at the producer level, and commercial activity is mostly in agriprocessing handled by a small number of SMEs (World Bank 2019).

At the end of October 2017, the government owned shares in 40 enterprises, 18 of which were majority owned (WTO 2018). The principal sectors concerned are mining, transport and transport support services, financial services, telecommunications, industry, agriculture, energy, and trade. Seven enterprises were holding monopoly positions in the mining, energy, transport, and trade sectors. Foreign investment, especially from China, has risen dramatically in recent years, as exemplified by China's decision in September 2017 to support Guinea's mining industry through a US$20 billion grant over a 20-year timeline in exchange for future mining concessions.

Barriers to entry and firm growth

Guinea's business environment not only imposes frictions on entry but also prevents firms that enter from reaching scale. Lack of infrastructure impedes market access; inefficient bureaucracy, weak rule of law, and political uncertainty increase risks; and lack of skilled workers hampers productivity. Of those challenges, market access tops the list: the inferior quality of Guinea's transport corridors is a main deterrent to nonmining private sector investments, including foreign ones.

Firms that enter have to face what is one of the most difficult operating environments in Africa. It takes 400 hours per year to file taxes for an average company in Guinea (versus 280 hours, on average, in the Sub-Saharan Africa region and 49 hours in Singapore), according to Doing Business indicators. Furthermore, the ratio of tax and contributions as a percentage of profit is 61.4 percent. These exceptionally high rates impose heavy burdens on firms, especially considering that firms are not necessarily receiving good public services in return. Also, a complicated tax system is associated with greater perceived corruption, less investment, and higher risks of evasion and informality, reducing revenue for the government. Similarly, goods take, on average, 52 days to export and 30 days to import, at a cost of US$906 for exports and US$989 for imports, ranking Guinea 167

FIGURE 4.5 Annual number of new firms registering in Guinea versus regional peers

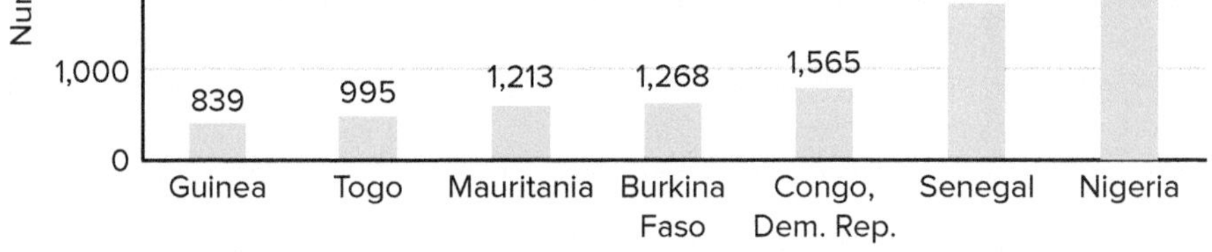

Source: Doing Business entrepreneurship data (2014).

globally on the Doing Business indicator for trading across borders, the second-lowest performer in the index.

This daunting business environment translates into low business density in the country and low penetration of large firms. Data collected in 2014 on Guinea's new business density ratio show that, with a few exceptions (Liberia, Niger, and São Tomé and Príncipe), Guinea trails most of its regional and global peers and struggles with low private sector dynamism, with only 0.13 new business registration per 1,000 working-age adults (figure 4.5).

The public sector approach: State-ownership and joint ventures

Efforts to create markets in Guinea have been secondary to turbulent politics and poorly implemented for decades. Successive governments have promoted state-owned enterprises to fill the gaps left by the lack of local private large firms (Nellis 2005). Some of the large enterprises operating in Guinea today—like the Guinean Oil Palm and Rubber Tree Company, which cultivates 22,000 hectares of plantations and employs more than 3,500 employees—originate from these policies (WTO 2018). The performance of state-owned firms generally fails to meet the expectations of their creators.

In recent years, policy has shifted toward creating public-private joint ventures. The Project to Develop the Cotton Subsector in Guinea, for example, was adopted in May 2011, creating a private company whose shares are held mostly by the state and Géocoton, a private company responsible for managing and providing technical support for the new venture. This project led to the establishment of a cotton-ginning plant. Production rose from 45,000 to 120,000 tons of cotton lint between 2011–12 and 2016–17, with annual exports of 10,000 tons of cotton lint, chiefly to Senegal. The Géocoton plant supplies inputs on credit to 17,000 cotton farmers, who are supervised by staff from the plant (WTO 2018).

How can the government facilitate large-firm creation today?

To boost private investment, the government of Guinea initiated pro-market reforms of its business and regulatory environment in 2013. These reforms included establishing new government institutions such as the Agency for Private Investment Promotion (APIP), enacting a new investment code in 2015, establishing a one-stop shop for licensing mining companies, passing a new public-private partnerships (PPPs) law in 2017, and establishing a new commercial court that is expected to improve the legal operating environment for firms. In 2018 alone, more than five reforms were recorded aimed at improving the business environment by facilitating market entry (by streamlining registration through a one-stop shop), property registration (by reducing property transfer fees), construction permitting (by reducing the cost and time to obtain a permit), international trade (by reducing inspection requirements), and contract enforcement (by adopting a law regulating mediation), among others (World Bank 2018c). In 2018, the reform momentum moved the country's position on the World Bank's Doing Business ranking to 152 (out of 190), up from 179 in 2012 (World Bank 2018c).

A range of reforms are still needed to support the entry of large firms. The first is to open markets to competition. The regulatory framework for competition and price control has not changed since 1994, and the country's competition authority is not fully operational (WTO 2018). The government could revise regulations or policies that (a) reinforce dominance or limit entry, (b) are conducive to collusive outcomes or increase costs to compete in the market, or (c) discriminate and protect vested interests. The second is to improve business entry (and exit), mainly by streamlining the business registration, licensing, and permitting process. By centralizing more procedures and removing the paid-in capital requirement, the government could replicate in other sectors the one-stop-shop model that was established to improve licensing in the mining sector. Streamlining licensing and using a risk-based approach for the licensing process would encourage new firms to enter the market and to access new sectors. In parallel, easing the conditions for firms' exit by introducing measures for insolvency proceedings would facilitate the exit of low-productivity firms. The third is to mobilize foreign investors. The recently enacted Investment Code regulating FDI, ratified in May 2015, remains to be implemented effectively. Slow implementation of the new PPP law is delaying the implementation of large PPP projects in transport, energy, water and sanitation, health, telecommunications, industrial parks, tourism, and mining that involve the creation of large firms.

Tackling the operational constraints of large firms is also essential to unlock the growth of new entrants. Several reforms could address these barriers. First, the commercial judicial system could be strengthened by operationalizing the new commercial court as well as building the capacity of the judiciary through the training and recruitment of new judges and clerks specialized in commercial law. Second, the tax payment system could be improved in numerous ways. Automating tax payments through an e-filing system and online payment systems would improve the efficiency of the tax system, especially for larger companies. In addition, digitizing the National Social Security system and connecting it with other agencies would facilitate filing and social contributions by employers. Third, skills are needed to enhance productivity in strategic sectors such as agriculture, where farmers lack the knowledge needed to increase productivity, as well as the financial sector, where low literacy has hindered the uptake and expansion of mobile money services. The lack of skills is even more acute in mining, where large-firm investment is high. Vocational training programs would go a long way in this direction.

Overall, strengthening accountability, governance, and the rule of law could greatly improve the operating environment for firms of all sizes. Actions could focus in the short term on creating private sector feedback loops and increasing government openness and transparency through accountability institutions and independent complaint mechanisms where firms can raise their concerns.

The role of development finance institutions

Development finance institutions (DFIs) can support countries' efforts to promote more large firms. Since the establishment of the International Finance Corporation (IFC) in 1956, DFIs have built up a long track record of investing in and building the capacity of large firms. In its early years, IFC financed mainly large foreign firms from high-income economies seeking to establish and expand operations in lower-income countries. The first loan in 1957, for example, was to support the expansion of German manufacturer Siemens' affiliate in Brazil to manufacture electrical equipment. Over time, IFC increased its support for medium and large firms from low- and middle-income countries, including support for cross-border expansion (so-called "south-south" investing) and support for established large firms to enter new industries. For example, Korea's LG Electronics began its international breakthrough with a US$17 million IFC loan-and-advice package in 1974 and soon became one of the first globally competitive firms from a lower-income country. Privatization programs of the 1990s also supported market creation around large firms in former planned economies,[4] an experience that has been applied since then to numerous African and Asian economies where privatizations were necessary to boost the development outcomes of large firms. Other DFIs have followed similar trajectories.

At the same time, in recognition of the lack of large firms in lower-income countries, DFIs have undertaken extensive financing and capacity-building activities to support entrepreneurship and the growth of high-potential SMEs. By partnering with many types of financial intermediaries—including microfinance institutions, commercial banks, and leasing companies—DFIs reach smaller firms indirectly with these objectives. After a first project in 1976 for Kenya Commercial Bank to on-lend to smaller local companies, in the second half of the 2010s about 20 percent of IFC loans were targeting SMEs and microenterprises.

Some of these efforts have exploited synergies with investments in large firms that have a broad base of SME suppliers, such as "linkage" programs that support the creation of value chains around DFI-financed large firms. IFC's support for value chain development includes top-down initiatives (tailored to the needs of large firms and working backward in their chain to build the capacity of SMEs), bottom-up initiatives (instruments customized to the needs of SMEs to position them as suppliers to larger firms), and industrywide action (often a combination of top-down and bottom-up initiatives and business-enabling environment reforms) (World Bank 2018a). They also involve the full range of instruments, from financing to technical assistance that helps suppliers meet the standards of larger producers, alleviating firm-specific constraints along value chains, while ensuring that smaller firms within and across industries benefit from their growth.

There are many examples of successful engagements of this kind, such as Bayer in the chemicals industry in Ukraine and Cargill in agriculture in Côte d'Ivoire, with an important impact. They all build on commercial return, mutual business advantages along the value chain, sufficient capacity of supply chain stakeholders to respond to business incentives, and a supportive, enabling environment.

DFIs with a global mandate like IFC play an important role in supporting the creation and growth of new, large firms in low- and middle-income countries. They can provide financing with a scale and tenor beyond that of local financial institutions; they can provide specialist advice, capacity building, and support to management; they can broker joint ventures and partnerships between firms; and they can help firms to achieve the quality standards needed to participate in global value chains. The ability of DFIs to form long-term partnerships can play an important role in helping new, large firms grow and prosper.

Notes

1 | For more information, see http://www.country-data.com/cgi-bin/query/r-12303.html.

2 | Abuse of market position can take place through various means, including pricing goods and services excessively, denying competitors access to essential supplies or facilities, engaging in price discrimination, and pricing goods and services below cost to exclude rivals.

3 | For more information, see https://www.lexafrica.com/developments-in-competition-law-in-africa/.

4 | In 1991 IFC supported Poland in designing its privatization program and launching the initial public offering of Swarzedzkie Fabryki Mebli, the first widely distributed retail initial public offering in post-communist Eastern Europe.

References

Amsden, Alice H., and Wan-Wen Chu. 2003. *Beyond Late Development*. Cambridge, MA: MIT Press.

Andrews, Dan, Chiara Criscuolo, and Peter N. Gal. 2016. "The Best Versus the Rest: The Global Productivity Slowdown, Divergence across Firms, and the Role of Public Policy." OECD Productivity Working Paper 05, OECD Publishing, Paris.

APIP (Agency for Private Investment Promotion). 2016. *Transformer le potentiel de la Guinée en prosperité pour le people Guinéen: 2016–2020*. Konakry: APIP.

Baumol, William J. 1982. "Contestable Markets: An Uprising in the Theory of Industrial Structure." *American Economic Review* 72 (1): 1–15.

Bloom, Nicholas, Benn Eifert, Aprajit Mahajan, David McKenzie, and John Roberts. 2013. "Does Management Matter? Evidence from India." *Quarterly Journal of Economics* 128 (1): 1–51.

Cherif, R., and F. Hasanov. 2019. "The Return of the Policy That Shall Not Be Named: Principles of Industrial Policy." IMF Working Paper 19/74, International Monetary Fund, Washington, DC.

Cirera, Xavier, and William F. Maloney. 2017. *The Innovation Paradox: Developing Country Capabilities and the Unrealized Promise of Technological Catch-Up*. Washington, DC: World Bank.

Comin, Diego, and Martí Mestieri. 2018. "If Technology Has Arrived Everywhere, Why Has Income Diverged?" *American Economic Journal: Macroeconomics* 10 (3): 137–78.

Criscuolo, Chiara, Ralf Martin, Henry Overman, and John Van Reenan. 2012. "The Causal Effects of an Industrial Policy." IZA Discussion Paper 6323, IZA Institute of Labor Economics, Bonn.

De Stefano, Timothy, Richard Kneller, and Jonathan Timmis. 2018. "Broadband Infrastructure, ICT Use, and Firm Performance: Evidence for UK Firms." *Journal of Economic Behavior and Organization* 155 (November): 110–39.

Doral, Murat, and Michael Patrono. 2010. "Chaebol and Korea's Industrial Finance." *Journal of Global Initiatives: Policy, Pedagogy, Perspective* 5 (2): Art. 7.

Freund, Caroline. 2016. *Rich People Poor Countries: The Rise of Emerging-Market Tycoons and Their Mega Firms*. Washington, DC: Peterson Institute for International Economics.

Hallward-Driemeier, Mary, and Lant Pritchett. 2015. "How Business Is Done in the Developing World: Deals versus Rules." *Journal of Economic Perspectives* 29 (3): 121–40.

Hoeckman, Bernard, and Peter S. Holmes. 1999. "Competition Policy, Developing Countries, and the WTO." FEEM Working Paper 66-99, Fondazione Eni Enrico Mattei, Milan.

Koske, Isabell, Isabelle Wanner, Rosamaria Bitetti, and Omar Barbiero. 2015. "The 2013 Update of the OECD Product Market Regulation Indicators: Policy Insights for OECD and Non-OECD Countries." OECD Economics Department Working Paper 1200, OECD Publishing, Paris.

Lejárraga, Iza, and Alexandros Ragoussis. 2018. "Beyond Capital: Monitoring Development Outcomes of Multinational Enterprises." Policy Research Working Paper 8686, World Bank, Washington, DC.

Munemo, Jonathan. 2015. "Foreign Direct Investment, Business Start-Up Regulations, and Entrepreneurship in Africa." *Economics Bulletin* 35 (1): n.p.

Naval Post-Graduate School. 2014. *The Institutional Rise of the Chaebols throughout South Korea's Transitional Vulnerabilities*. Scotts Valley, CA: CreateSpace Independent Publishing Platform.

Nellis, John. 2005. "The Evolution of Enterprise Reform in Africa: From State-Owned Enterprises to Private Participation in Infrastructure—and Back?" ESMAP Technical Paper 084, World Bank, Washington, DC.

Schwab, Klaus. 2019. *The Global Competitiveness Report 2019*. Geneva: World Economic Forum.

Siddiqi, Moin. 2016. "Sierra Leone Looks to FDI to Jump-Start the Economy." Developing Markets Associates (blog). https://www.developingmarkets.com/perspectives/sierra-leone-looks-fdi -jumpstart-economy.

Stiglitz, Joseph E. 1987. "Technological Change, Sunk Costs, and Competition." *Brookings Papers on Economic Activity* 3: 883–937.

United Nations. 2019. *World Investment Report 2019*. Geneva: United Nations Conference on Trade and Development.

World Bank. 2016. *Breaking Down Barriers: Unlocking Africa's Potential through Vigorous Competition Policy*. Washington, DC: World Bank.

World Bank. 2018a. *Doing Business 2019*. Washington, DC: World Bank.

World Bank. 2018b. *Global Competitiveness Report 2017–2018*. Washington, DC: World Bank.

World Bank. 2018c. *Partnership for Growth: Linking Large Firms and Agro-Processing SMEs*. Washington, DC: World Bank.

World Bank. 2019. "Guinea Country Private Sector Diagnostic (CPSD)." World Bank, Washington, DC.

World Bank. 2020. *Global Competitiveness Report 2019–2020*. Washington, DC: World Bank.

World Bank. Various years. Doing Business database. Washington, DC: World Bank.

World Bank. Various years. Enterprise Survey database. Washington, DC: World Bank.

World Economic Forum. Various years. Global Investment Competitiveness database. Geneva: World Economic Forum.

WTO (World Trade Organization). 2018. "Trade Policy Review Report by the WTO Secretariat: Guinea." WT/TPR/S/370, WTO Secretariat, Geneva, April 2018.

Appendixes

Appendix A: Methodology for large-firm premiums

Using establishment-level data from the World Bank Enterprise Surveys, we examine the ways in which large establishments are different from smaller and medium-size ones according to their characteristics, actions, and experiences and across several measures of performance. For consistency with the rest of the study, we refer to these differences between large and smaller establishments as large-firm premiums.

As a first step, we look at the difference between large and smaller establishments, controlling for only country and sector of operation. In this first step, we are comparing the average characteristics and outcomes of large and smaller establishments, without taking into account any other characteristics associated with being large. This average premium is estimated via the following ordinary least squares regression:

$$y_{isc} = \beta_0 + \beta_L \cdot Large_i + D_c + D_s + \varepsilon_{isc},$$

FIGURE A.1 Innovation: Bundled premiums for 100+ and 300+ firms

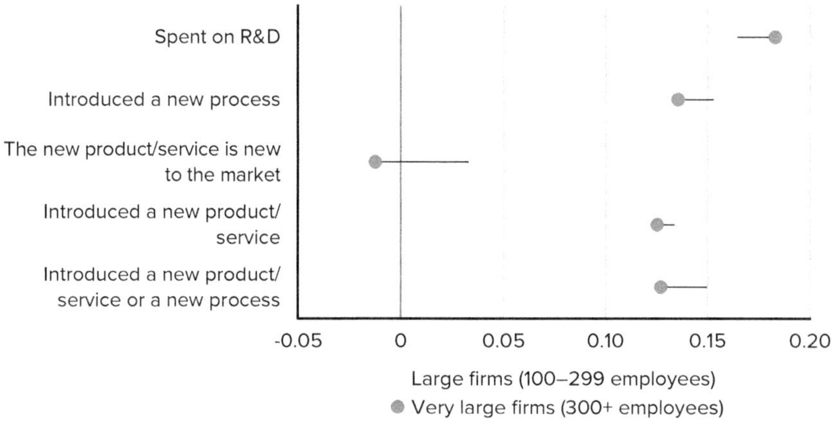

Source: Calculations based on World Bank Enterprise Survey data.
Note: R&D = research and development.

where, y_{isc} is the outcome (that is, characteristic, action, experience, or measure of performance) for establishment i operating in sector s and country c; $large_i$ is a dummy variable indicating whether establishment i is large; β_L is the estimated large-firm premium; D_C and D_S are country and sector fixed effects (dummy variables); and ε_{isc} represents the error term.

In the next step, we reestimate the large-firm premium, this time accounting for a range of establishment-level characteristics that may also be associated with being large and that are likely to be related to establishments' observed outcomes. These characteristics are age, foreign ownership, multiple-establishment status, exporting status, the top manager's experience in the sector, the establishment's legal form, and the establishment's size at birth. These characteristics are contained in the vector X_i in the following equation:

$$y_{isc} = \gamma_0 + \gamma_L \cdot large_i + D_C + D_S + \gamma_i \cdot X_i + \varepsilon_{isc}.$$

The term γ_L represents the premium associated with being large, after taking other establishment-level characteristics into account.

Reference

World Bank. Various years. Enterprise Surveys database. Washington, DC: World Bank.

Appendix B: The OECD Orbis database

The Organisation for Economic Co-operation and Development (OECD) Orbis database is the largest available cross-country company-level database for economic and financial research. The database contains annual balance sheet and income statements, commercial data collected by Bureau van Dijk—an electronic publishing firm—using a variety of underlying sources ranging from credit-rating agencies (such as Cerved in Italy) to national banks (National Bank of Belgium for Belgium) as well as financial information providers (Thomson Reuters for the United States).

The OECD Orbis database is a version of the database that has been treated by the OECD for the purposes of economic analysis, using three steps. The steps follow suggestions by Kalemli-Ozcan et al. (2015) and previous OECD experience (Gal 2013; Pinto Ribeiro, Menghinello, and Backer 2010) and include (a) ensuring the comparability of monetary variables across countries and over time (industry-level purchasing power parity conversion and deflation), (b) deriving new variables for analytical purposes (capital stock, productivity), and (c) keeping company accounts with valid and relevant information for present purposes (filtering or cleaning). For most countries, the OECD Orbis includes a subsample of the universe of companies, with smaller firms often being underrepresented.

Four country samples have been retained for the purposes of this report: France, Italy, Spain, and Sweden in 2012 (figure B.1). All business sectors of the

FIGURE B.1 Large-firm premiums in high-income versus low- and middle-income countries

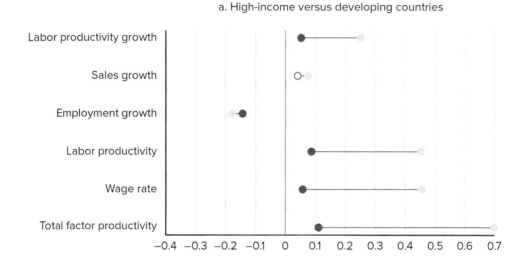

a. High-income versus developing countries

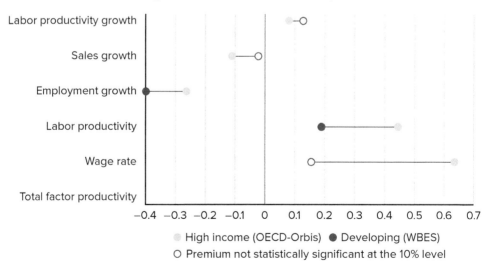

b. High-income countries, Eastern Europe: OECD-Orbis versus WBES

Sources: Calculations based on World Bank Enterprise Survey (WBES) data and OECD Orbis data
Note: Total factor productivity estimated for manufacturing firms (excluding petroleum manufacturing) with more than 20 employees using the instrumental variables method proposed by Wooldridge (2009). This figure presents the coefficient on large-firm binary variables in a series of linear ordinary least square regressions with each performance indicator as a dependent variable, and controls for country and sector fixed effects.

economy are covered (excluding government services). The sample includes up to 1.4 million firms in four countries, with 24,000 employing 100+ workers (2 percent of the sample).

References

Gal, Peter N. 2013. "Measuring Productivity at the Firm Level Using ORBIS." OECD Economics Department Working Paper 1049, OECD Publishing, Paris.

Kalemli-Ozcan, Sebnem, Bent Sorensen, Carolina Villegas-Sanchez, Vadym Volosovych, and Sevcan Yesiltas. 2015. "How to Construct Nationally Representative Firm Level Data from the ORBIS Global Database." NBER Working Paper 21558, National Bureau of Economic Research, Cambridge, MA.

OECD (Organisation for Economic Co-operation and Development). Various years. Orbis database. Paris: OECD.

Pinto Ribeiro, Samuel, Stefano Menghinello, and Koen De Backer. 2010. "The OECD ORBIS Database: Responding to the Need for Firm-Level Micro-Data in the OECD." OECD Statistics Working Paper 2010/01, OECD Publishing, Paris.

Wooldridge, Jeffrey M. 2009. "On Estimating Firm-Level Production Functions Using Proxy Variables to Control for Unobservables." *Economics Letters* 104 (3): 112–14.

Appendix C: Why is the large-firm wage premium higher in lower-income countries?

FIGURE C.1 Large-firm wage premium and labor rights, by country

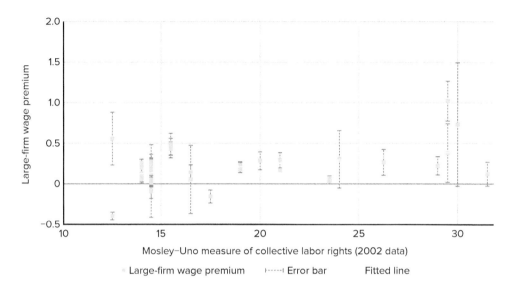

Mosley–Uno measure of collective labor rights (2002 data)

Large-firm wage premium ⊢-----⊣ Error bar Fitted line

Source: Calculations based on World Bank International Income Distribution Data Set (I2D2) data (2018).
Note: Large-firm premium is estimated at the country level in Mincer regressions, controlling for occupation and industry.

TABLE C.1 Large-firm wage premium regressions

	Log hourly wage	Log hourly wage	Log hourly wage	Log hourly wage
Large-firm (100+ employees)	0.363***	0.245 ***	0.216***	0.146***
	(0.000)	(0.000)	(0.000)	(0.000)
Other controls:				
Country fixed effects	Yes	Yes	Yes	Yes
Year fixed effects	Yes	Yes	Yes	Yes
Sector fixed effects	Yes			
Mincer controls (age, gender, marital status, education sector fixed effects)		Yes	Yes	Yes
Occupation fixed effects			Yes	
Contract				Yes
Social security				Yes
Health benefits				Yes
M	969,421	635,266	599,495	215,574
R^2	0.788	0.S17	0.S20	0.869

Source: Calculations based on World Bank International Income Distribution Data Set (I2D2) data (2018).
Note: Results from regressing lag wage on large-firm dummy in a pooled sample of 26 countries.
*$p < .10$ ** $p < .05$ *** $p < .01$..

Appendix D: Outliers of the firm distribution

TABLE D.1 Difference in means, labor productivity outliers

Characteristic	Productivity outlier	Not productivity outlier	T-test difference in means
Employment	144.57	46.39	98.18***
	(705.35)	(373.839)	74.99
Exporting firm	0.217	0.114	0.103***
	(0.412)	(0.318)	83.30
Importing firm	0.538	0.313	0.225***
	(0.499)	(0.464)	63.10
Observations	2,011,065		

Standard deviation in parentheses. *$p < .10$ **$p < .05$ ***$p < .01$.

TABLE D.2 Difference in means, sales outliers

Characteristic	Sales outlier	Not sales outlier	*T*-test difference in means
Employment	391.24	29.97	361.27***
	(1341.96)	(218.51)	311.74
Exporting firm	0.278	0.106	0.172***
	(0.448)	(0.308)	161.73
Importing firm	0.593	0.302	0.291***
	(0.491)	(0.459)	98.77
Observations	2,011,065		

Source: Calculations based on business census data for Côte d'Ivoire, Ethiopia, Indonesia, and Serbia.
Note: Manufacturing data were collected for as many years as possible for each country from 2000 to 2012, while service data were collected for the year closest to 2007. Countries were identified as high income following the World Bank Income Classifications 2017.
Standard deviation in parentheses. $^*p < .10$ $^{**}p < .05$ $^{***}p < .01$.

TABLE D.3 Predicted versus actual share of employment in large firms in selected higher- and lower-income countries

Country	Period	*k*	0–30 workers	31–299 workers	300+ workers
Côte d'Ivoire	2003–13	1.07	−0.088	+0.015	−0.060
Ethiopia	2000–11	1.07	−0.135	+0.225	−0.094
Indonesia	2009–15	1.04	−0.094	+0.160	−0.063
Serbia	2006–15	1.12	−0.012	+0.210	−0.089
Vietnam	2007–12	1.11	−0.085	+0.015	−0.063
South Africa	2012–14	1.16	−0.03	+0.044	−0.014

Source: Calculations based on business census data for Côte d'Ivoire, Ethiopia, Indonesia, Serbia, South Africa, and Vietnam.
Note: Median values are reported. The Industrial Censuses for Ethiopia and Indonesia only cover the manufacturing sector.

Appendix E:
IFC client data

TABLE E.1 Information collected from International Finance Corporation (IFC) appraisal documents

Variable	Format text	Source project characteristics
ID	Numerical	Project characteristics
Country	3-digit ISIC	Project characteristics
Industry	2 Digit ISIC Rev 4	Project characteristics
Industry (secondary)	2 Digit ISIC Rev 4	Project characteristics
Size (Last record)	Ordinal [S, M, L]	Project characteristics
Year (Last record)	Numerical	Project characteristics
MINE	O/1	IRM book/company
Family owned	O/1	IRM book/company
Year founded	Numerical	IRM book/company
Orgin size (estimate)	Ordinal [S, M, L]	IRM book/company
Orgin sector	2 Digit ISIC Rev 4	IRM book/company
Sponser's nationality: Domestic	O/1	IRM book/company
Sponser's sole venture: Yes	O/1	IRM book/company
Sponser's gender: Woman	O/1	IRM book/company
Sponser's public status: Listed	O/1	IRM book/company
Sponser's type: State	O/1	IRM book/company
Orgin event: technological development	O/1	IRM book/company

(continued)

TABLE E.1 *Continued*

Variable	Format text	Source project characteristics
Orgin event: regulatory change	O/1	IRM book/company
Orgin event: world market shock	O/1	IRM book/company
Orgin event: merger (market consolidation)	O/1	IRM book/company
Management: previous management experience in same sector	O/1	IRM book/company
Management: previous management experience in another sector	2 Digit ISIC Rev 4	IRM book/company
Management: previous management experience in other large companies	O/1	IRM book/company
Market served: new product/service	O/1	IRM book/company
Market served: intermediate product/service	O/1	IRM book/company
Market served: foreign market	O/1	IRM book/company
Market served: social/public service	O/1	IRM book/company
Finance: reinvested earnings	O/1	IRM book/company
Finance: loans	O/1	IRM book/company
Finance: equity	O/1	IRM book/company
Growth strategy: foreign expansion	O/1	IRM book/company
Growth strategy: product/service expansion	O/1	IRM book/company
Growth strategy: vertical integration	O/1	IRM book/company
Assets: intangibles (latest year)	Numerical [US$]	Financial statements
Assets: property, plan and equipment (latest year)	Numerical [US$]	Financial statements
Turnover (latest year)	Numerical [US$]	Financial statements
Value added (latest year)	Numerical [US$]	Financial statements
Employees (latest year)	Numerical [US$]	Financial statements
Share of market (latest year) > 50 percent	O/1	Financial statements
Exporter	O/1	Financial statements
Exporter turnover	Numerical [US$]	Financial statements
Wage bill (latest year)	Numerical [US$]	Financial statements
Expected development impact: economic	O/1	IRM book
Expected development impact: social	O/1	IRM book
Expected development impact: environmental	O/1	IRM book

Source: International Finance Corporation.
Note: ISIC = International Standard Industrial Classification.

FIGURE E.1 Sectoral composition of International Finance Corporation (IFC)–appraised firms

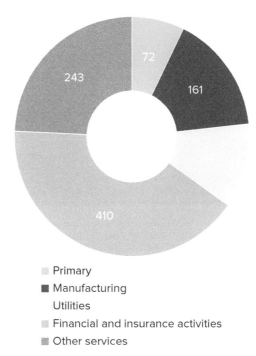

- Primary
- Manufacturing
- Utilities
- Financial and insurance activities
- Other services

Source: International Finance Corporation.

Appendix F: Origin and growth path results

FIGURE F.1   Number of large manufacturing and services firms in Kosovo and
Moldova, 2004–15

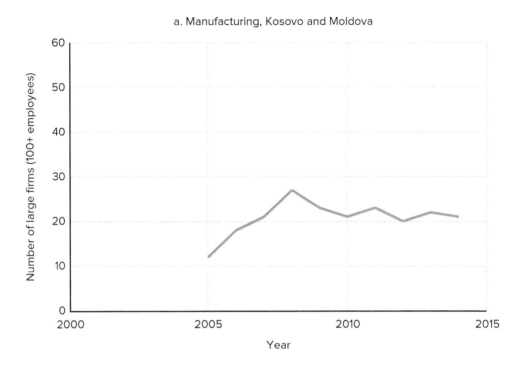

a. Manufacturing, Kosovo and Moldova

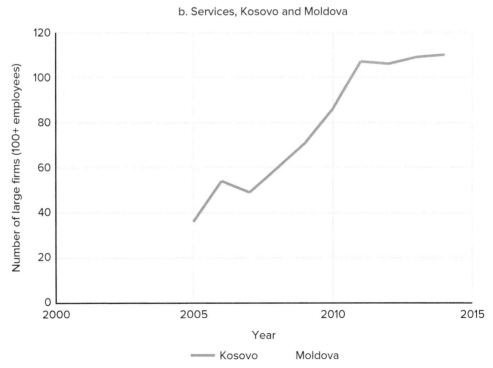

b. Services, Kosovo and Moldova

TABLE F.1 Why do firms start large?

Characteristic	Start size (log employment)	Start size (log employment)	Start large	Start large
Dependence on external finance	−0.0899***	−1.710**	−0.00903***	0.0288
	(0.000)	(0.001)	(0.000)	(0.712)
Lagged average size of incumbents (minimum efficiency scale proxy)	0.00271***	0.00272***	0.000267***	0.000270***
	(0.000)	(0.000)	(0.000)	(0.000)
Lagged gross exit rate in the industry (sunk cost proxy)	−1.028***	−1.042***	0.00231	0.00247
	(0.000)	(0.000)	(0.742)	(0.724)
Herfindahl-Hirschman Index (sales)	−0.198***	−0.182***	−0.0126**	−0.00990*
	(0.000)	(0.000)	(0.002)	(0.015)
Foreign owned	0.223***	0.223***	0.0103***	0.0102***
	(0.000)	(0.000)	(0.000)	(0.000)
Lagged industry sales growth	−0.000257***	−0.000253***	−0.0000556***	−0.0000540***
	(0.000)	(0.000)	(0.000)	(0.000)
Country fixed effects	Yes	Yes	Yes	Yes
Country fixed effects*external finance	No	Yes	No	Yes
Sector fixed effects	Yes	Yes	Yes	Yes
Year fixed effects	Yes	Yes	Yes	Yes

Source: World Bank calculations based on Orbis data.
Note: Large refers to firms with at least 100 employees. Dependence on external finance is calculated using Orbis data for firms in the United States. It is defined as the industry-level (two-digit ISIC rev.4 sector level) median ratio of capital expenditure minus cash flow over capital expenditure, following the methodology used by Rajan and Zingales (1998). We keep only country samples whose industry classification can be mapped to ISIC rev.4. Hence the sample excludes China. All lagged variables are calculated as a three-year average at the two-digit industry level. ISIC = International Standard Industrial Classification. Standard deviations are in parentheses.
*$p < .10$ ** $p < .05$ *** $p < .01$.

References

OECD (Organisation for Economic Co-operation and Development). Various years. Orbis database. Paris: OECD.

Rajan, Raghuram G., and Luigi Zingales. 1998. "Financial Dependence and Growth." *American Economic Review* 88 (3): 559–86.

Appendix G: Sample for the growth path analysis

The growth path analysis studies key variables regarding size, labor productivity, markets, financing, investment, and organizational structure. For all monetary variables, we use the gross domestic product (GDP) deflator to construct real values.

As a consequence of the nature of our data set, the variable definitions are not always homogeneous across countries. Employment can explicitly include seasonal employees (Côte d'Ivoire) or exclude them (Morocco). It can be measured at a particular time of the year (Ethiopia and Vietnam) or averaged over the period (Serbia). In the case of Indonesia, it includes unpaid workers and excludes external and nonmanufacturing workers. Likewise, wages can capture wages and salaries including other benefits and contributions (Moldova, Morocco, and Serbia) or explicitly excluding them (China, Côte d'Ivoire, Ethiopia, Indonesia, and Vietnam).

TABLE G.1 Information availability in industrial censuses

Characteristic	Definitions	Note
Size	Employment and sales	Not available for all years for China and Kosovo.
Labor productivity	Value added/employment Sales/employment	Not available for Kosovo. Not available for all years for China and Vietnam. Not available for all years for China and Kosovo.
Markets	Becoming multiproduct	Not available for Ethiopia, Kosovo, Moldova, Morocco, and Serbia. Not available for all years for Indonesia.
	Becoming exporter	Not available for Moldova. Not available for all years for Kosovo.
Financing	Liability/total assets	Not available for China, Ethiopia, Indonesia, Kosovo, Morocco, and Serbia.
Investment	Fixed assets and Investment in fixed assets	Not available for China, Ethiopia, Kosovo, and Morocco. Not available for all years for Vietnam.
Organizational structure	Employment layers average wage	Only available for Côte d'Ivoire. Not available for Kosovo.

Source: World Bank.

We define capital as the book value of total fixed assets reported on the firm's balance sheet. International comparisons of levels of capital are difficult to make because data sources are susceptible to problems of international comparability. First, differences in capital cost and measurement of price indexes are a cause of potential bias. Second, the composition of capital can vary, even with the same book value of capital. For example, the treatment of many types of intangible assets such as software can be a leading cause of divergence in capital input measures across different accounting systems (see, for example, Ahmad 2004). When different types of capital can have different degrees of intrinsic efficiency and complementarities with other inputs, differences in capital composition alone can account for differences in labor productivity (Caselli and Wilson 2004).

Another caveat is the incomplete coverage of key variables. Table G.1 provides a summary of the availability of key variables across the sample countries. As a consequence, each growth path presented is based on a different subset of countries.

References

Ahmad, Nadim. 2004. "Introducing Capital Services into the Production Account." Paper presented at the meeting of the Canberra Group, Washington, DC.

Caselli, Francesco, and Daniel J. Wilson. 2004. "Importing Technology." *Journal of Monetary Economics* 51 (January): 1–32.

Appendix H: Growth paths for France

FIGURE H.1   Growth paths for France

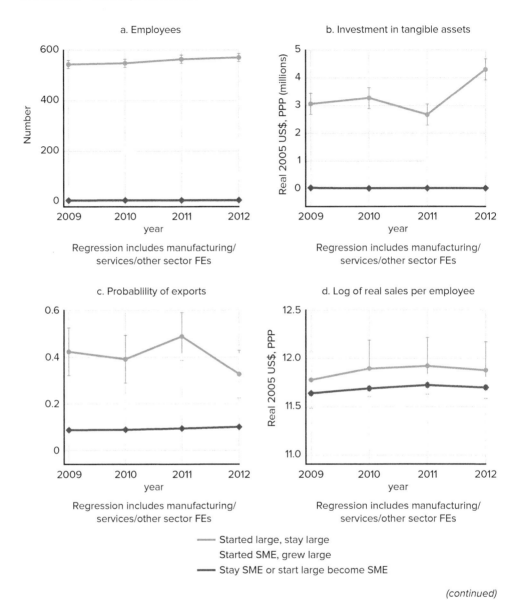

Regression includes manufacturing/
services/other sector FEs

Started large, stay large
Started SME, grew large
Stay SME or start large become SME

(continued)

FIGURE H.1 *Continued*

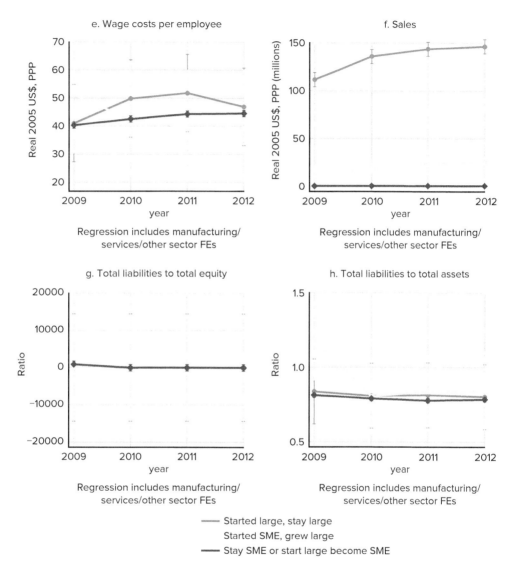

e. Wage costs per employee

f. Sales

g. Total liabilities to total equity

h. Total liabilities to total assets

Regression includes manufacturing/
services/other sector FEs

Regression includes manufacturing/
services/other sector FEs

Regression includes manufacturing/
services/other sector FEs

Regression includes manufacturing/
services/other sector FEs

Started large, stay large
Started SME, grew large
Stay SME or start large become SME

Source: OECD calculations based on OECD-Orbis data.
Note: The regressions include manufacturing, services, and other sector fixed effects (FEs). PPP = purchasing power parity.
SME = small and medium enterprise.